Remember Me
For My Football

To the memory of George Best.
(22nd May 1946 – 25th November 2005)

© 2012 Phil Hughes and Paul Collier

Published by The Bluecoat Press, Liverpool
Book design by March Design, Liverpool
Printed by GPS Colour Graphics, Belfast
Cover photo courtesy of Colorsport Ltd

ISBN 9781908457097

Acknowledgements Rob Bishop, Tony Bluff, Bognor Regis Library, Stuart Bolton, Martin Brodersky, Malcolm Brodie, Garry Brooke, Jim Brown, Cliff Butler, Peter Byrne, Chris Caldwell, Colin Cameron, Martin Chivers, Trevor Clydesdale, Paul Collins, Roy Conner, David Cooke, Paul Cooke, Denis Clarebrough, Andy Crossley, Matt Davies, Devonport City Soccer Club, Dave Dolan, Paul Dutton, Vidar Edell, Janet Elliott, Eifion Evans, Foxhall United (in memory of Graham Brooking), Ken Furphy, Steve Gordos, Tommy Guthrie, David Hall, Tony 'Reckless' Hammond, Steve Hardwick, Mary Hart, Ottar Felix Hauksson, Stuart Hayton, Steve Hobin, Phil Hollow, The Hong Kong Football Association, Alan Hutchinson, David Instone, Irish & Local Studies Library – Armagh, Willie Irvine, Gary James, Ian King, Richard Lambert, Lewes Library, Darren Lovell, Malachy McAleese, Iain McCartney, Gareth McCullogh, Helen McIntyre, Thomas McKenna (Junior), Tom McLellan, Sharon McQuillan, Bill McMurdo, Simon Marland, Dick Mattrick, Keith Mecalfe, Les Millman, Dave Morrison, John Neil Munro, Graham Oates, Mike Odgers, Roger Palmer, Tony Park, Ron Parrott, Andy Porter, Priaulx Library (Guernsey), Bryan Reed, Chris Reeves, Chris Rogers, Jeff Rourke, David Sadler, Kelly Scott, Steve Shirley, Neil Springate, John Staff, Staff and readers of the Mearns Leader (Stonehaven), San Jose Public Library, Swindon Collection – Swindon Central Library, David Tavener, Donald Taylor, Rupert Taylor, The Telford Journal, Jimmy Troake, Dennis Turner, Lars Ugland, Patrick Van Dort, Jane Viglietti, Brian Walder, Warwickshire Library & Information Service (Nuneaton Library), Roger Wash, Mark Watterson, Anne Wheeldon, Lester Wood, Tom Wright. Special thanks to Marion Collier for her endless encouragement.

Remember Me For My Football

George Best: For the Record

Phil Hughes
& Paul Collier

THE BLUECOAT PRESS

CONTENTS

2012 Foreword by Phil Hughes … … … … … … … … … … … … … … … 5

1961 / 62 Manchester United … … … … … … … … … … … … … … … 6

1962 / 63 Manchester United … … … … … … … … … … … … … … …8

1963 / 64 Manchester United … … … … … … … … … … … … …10

1964 / 65 Manchester United … … … … … … … … … … … … …14

1965 / 66 Manchester United … … … … … … … … … … … … …18

1966 / 67 Manchester United … … … … … … … … … … … …22

1967 / 68 Manchester United … … … … … … … … … … … …26

1968 / 69 Manchester United … … … … … … … … … … … …30

1969 / 70 Manchester United … … … … … … … … … … … …34

1970 / 71 Manchester United … … … … … … … … … … … …38

1971 / 72 Manchester United … … … … … … … … … … … …42

1972 / 73 Manchester United … … … … … … … … … … … …46

1973 / 74 Manchester United … … … … … … … … … … … …48

1974 Jewish Guild … … … … … … … … … … … … … … … …50

1974 / 75 Friendlies … … … … … … … … … … … … … … …51

1975 / 76 Stockport County … … … … … … … … … … … …52

1975 / 76 Friendlies … … … … … … … … … … … … … …54

1975 / 76 Cork Celtic … … … … … … … … … … … … …55

1976 Los Angeles Aztecs … … … … … … … … … … … …56

1976 / 77 Fulham … … … … … … … … … … … … … …58

1977 Los Angeles Aztecs … … … … … … … … … … …62

1977 / 78 Fulham … … … … … … … … … … … … … …64

1978 Los Angeles Aztecs … … … … … … … … … … …66

1978 Fort Lauderdale Strikers … … … … … … … … …67

1979 Fort Lauderdale Strikers … … … … … … … …68

1979 / 80 Hibernian … … … … … … … … … … … …70

1980 San Jose Earthquakes … … … … … … … … … …72

1980 / 81 Hibernian … … … … … … … … … … … …74

1980 / 81 + 1981 San Jose Earthquakes … … … … …76

1981 / 82 San Jose Earthquakes … … … … … … … …78

1982 / 83 AFC Bournemouth … … … … … … … … …80

1983 Brisbane Lions … … … … … … … … … … … …82

1984 Tobermore United … … … … … … … … … … …84

1970 – 76 Daily Express five-a-side Football … … … …84

1984 / 85 Friendlies … … … … … … … … … … … …86

1985 / 86 Friendlies … … … … … … … … … … … …87

1986 / 87 + 1987 / 88 Friendlies … … … … … … … …88

1988 / 89 + 1989 / 90 Friendlies … … … … … … … …89

1969 – 94 Friendly, Testimonial & Exhibition games … … … … … …90

1962 Northern Ireland Youth Internationals … … … … … … … …100

1964 – 77 Northern Ireland Internationals … … … … … … … …101

1971 – 74 The George Best Club … … … … … … … … …104

1946 – 2005 Miscellany … … … … … … … … … … … … …106

1961 – 84 Appearances … … … … … … … … … … … … …108

1961 – 84 Goals … … … … … … … … … … … … … …110

2012 Bibliography … … … … … … … … … … … … … …112

FOREWORD

My association with George began in 1986. It commenced with a chance meeting in Blondes in London's Mayfair. George promoted the club and I managed and ran a knitwear shop in west London. Somehow we got chatting and seemed to hit it off and it wasn't long before George asked for some business advice. Our friendship grew as did George's trust in me. A couple of years later he asked me if I would be his agent and I readily agreed. It was the beginning of a working relationship and friendship that lasted until his sad passing in November 2005.

George and I travelled the world together attending different events and functions. His playing career might have been long past but his popularity remained undiminished. Wherever we went, people across the globe wanted to talk football with him. Fans would recall games he had played in or goals he had scored. Often George would listen to similar stories from different people across the globe but he never tired of hearing them. He was happy just to know that his playing career had given so many people such immense pleasure.

Some 15 years ago I was introduced to Paul Collier. He was a George Best fan and his knowledge was astonishing. He seemed familiar with ever aspect of George's life and career and this detail put him in a league of his own. I mentioned Paul to George and we felt that we must get him on board to work with us on George's autobiography *Blessed* and its follow up, *Scoring at Half Time*. Whenever George was unclear about any aspect of his own life, he always suggested that we should phone Paul for clarification. George even joked that Paul knew more his life than he did!

Paul and I were talking one day and we thought it would be a wonderful project to put together the definitive book about George's playing career. No book had ever detailed his entire career in football. George was excited by the idea but realized the huge amount of work required. He wasn't wrong. Paul and I went away to plan the book and then spent countless months bringing it to life.

We are indebted to the many people who helped us with this book and gave their time so freely. Whether those who assisted were associated with big clubs like Manchester United or Fulham or smaller ones like Falmouth Town or Crewe United, all had nothing but nice memories and kind words to say about George.

I have lost count of the number of times in the last seven years that I have been approached by people wanting me to reveal every facet of my 25-year friendship and working relationship with George. Perhaps one day the time will be right but this book takes priority. After all, it relates to George's first love, football. From his first game in Manchester United's A team through to the numerous friendly and testimonial matches which he appeared at the end of his career, this book covers them all. I sincerely hope that Paul and I have done George proud. He told me several times that, ultimately, he wanted people to 'remember me for my football'. I can vouch that his legion of fans the world over will do just that.

Phil Hughes

George Best's first competitive game in a Manchester United shirt came on 9th September 1961 in a Lancashire League Division 1 fixture. He was 15 when he played for the A team in a 2-1 home win against Stockport County A. Two weeks later he made his first appearance in the B team in a Lancashire League Division 2 home match against Oldham Athletic A. United won the game 2-0. George scored his first competitive goal on 30th September 1961 when he netted once in a 5-1 away victory at Bury B. United's B team won three of their remaining six fixtures in 1961 before resounding away victories at Manchester City B and Bury B at the turn of the year. On 20th January 1962 George scored two more goals as United's B team beat Rochdale A 10-1. He netted in the next two B team matches in defeats against Blackpool B and Oldham Athletic A. On 17th February George played for the A team in a 7-0 home win against Stockport County A before switching back to the B team and playing in a 1-1 draw against Liverpool B the following Saturday.

On 3rd March 1962 he played again for the A team in a 4-2 home defeat against Blackpool B. Home games for the B team followed with a 4-0 defeat against Everton B and a 3-3 draw against Rochdale A. Best scored once in a 2-0 home win versus Bolton Wanderers B and two more in a 5-0 home victory against Rochdale A the following week. On 7th April 1962 the B team beat Blackburn Rovers 5-2 away and then triumphed 2-1 against Manchester City B five days later. George then scored two more goals playing for the A team in a 3-1 away win at Everton A before appearing for the side in a 2-0 home defeat against Liverpool A. George's season was concluded in the B team when he scored in a 4-0 away win at Burnley B and a 2-0 home victory against Bolton Wanderers B. Best's first season at Old Trafford saw him play 27 times for the junior sides and score 12 goals.

Below Probable (though unconfirmed) first competitive game for Manchester United, 5th September 1961.

Below right Team page Manchester United Youth XI v A Selected XI.

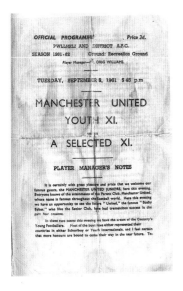

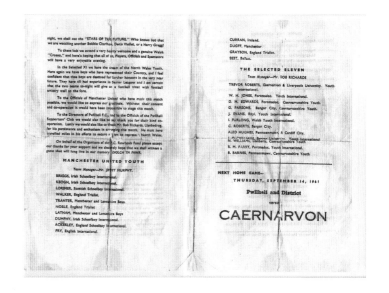

A TEAM LANCASHIRE LEAGUE DIVISION 1

			Shirt	Goals	Score
1. 9th September 1961 (SC)	Stockport County A	H	8		2-1
2. 17th February 1962	Stockport County A	H	8		7-0
3. 3rd March 1962	Blackpool A	H	7		2-4
4. 14th April 1962	Everton A	A	8	2	3-1
5. 17th April 1962	Liverpool A	H	8		0-2

B TEAM LANCASHIRE LEAGUE DIVISION 2

			Shirt	Goals	Score
1. 23rd September 1961 (SC)	Oldham Athletic A	H	8		2-0
2. 30th September 1961 (SC)	Bury B	A	8	1	5-1
3. 7th October 1961	Tranmere Rovers A	A	8		3-1
4. 14th October 1961	Bury B	H	7		1-0
5. 28th October 1961 (SC)	Manchester City B	A	8		1-2
6. 11th November 1961	Oldham Athletic A	A	8		1-4
7. 18th November 1961	Burnley B	H	8		2-0
8. 25th November 1961	Blackburn Rovers B	H	8		1-1
9. 6th January 1962	Manchester City B	A	7		4-2
10. 13th January 1962	Bury B	A	8		4-0
11. 20th January 1962	Rochdale A	A	8	2	10-1
12. 27th January 1962	Blackpool B	A	8	1	2-3
13. 10th February 1962	Oldham Athletic A	H	8	1	1-2
14. 24th February 1962	Liverpool B	A	7		1-1
15. 10th March 1962	Everton B	H	8		0-4
16. 17th March 1962	Rochdale A	H	8		3-3
17. 24th March 1962	Bolton Wanderers B	H	8	1	2-0
18. 31st March 1962 (SC)	Rochdale A	H	10	2	5-0
19. 7th April 1962	Blackburn Rovers B	A	8		5-2
20. 12th April 1962	Manchester City B	H	8		2-1
21. 28th April 1962	Burnley B	A	7	1	4-0
22. 30th April 1962	Bolton Wanderers B	H	8	1	2-0

SC = Supplementary Competition

George began the new season in the B team playing in a 2-0 home defeat against Burnley B. He scored in the next match, also against Burnley B but away in a 5-2 loss. A 6-0 victory on 1st September 1962 against Manchester City B followed before Best netted again in a 4-3 victory at Burnley B. On 29th September 1962 Bury B were defeated 5-0 at home and then George scored five goals in the next three games against Rochdale A at home and away to Bolton Wanderers B and Rochdale A. These games were followed with a 2-1 win against Bury B at home and a 2-2 draw away to Everton before Best scored twice for the A team in a 3-0 away victory at Preston North End. Two wins and a defeat followed before George again appeared for the B team on Boxing Day. Blackburn Rovers B were defeated with Best scoring the only goal of the game.

On 23rd February 1963 the B team drew 1-1 at home to Oldham Athletic A before George netted eight goals in the following three games. He scored two in a 8-2 win at Bury B, four in a 7-0 victory at Manchester City B and two more in a 3-0 home win against Bolton Wanderers B. On 23rd March 1963 the Irishman scored twice for the A team in a 4-2 loss at Burnley B before scoring for the B team the following week in a 2-2 draw against Everton B. On 6th April 1963 Best scored once for the A team in a 8-2 rout at home to Preston North End A. He played in a 2-1 away victory against Tranmere Rovers A and a 1-1 draw at Blackpool A. George converted two more goals in a 4-2 win against Tranmere Rovers A before playing for the youth team for the first time in a 3-0 home win against Newcastle United. On 27th April 1963 he appeared for the A team in a 6-4 away win at Liverpool A before playing again for the youth team in a 2-0 loss at Sheffield Wednesday three days later. Best's season was concluded when he scored two goals for the B team in a 4-0 home win against Manchester City B and finally for the B side in a 2-0 loss at Oldham Athletic A.

The 1962 / 63 season saw George Best play 28 games for the junior sides and score 26 goals plus appear in a further two FA Youth Cup matches without scoring.

FA Youth Cup debut versus Newcastle United, 24th April 1963.

Second Appearance in FA Youth Cup versus Sheffield Wednesday, 30th April 1963.

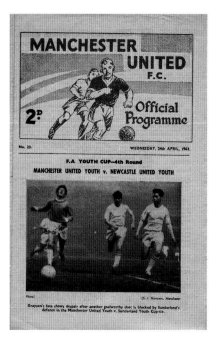

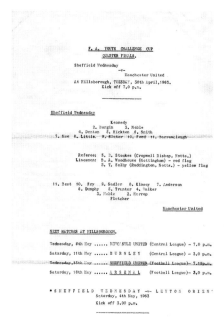

A TEAM – LANCASHIRE LEAGUE DIVISION 1

			Shirt	Goals	Score
1. 24th November 1962	Preston North End A	A	10	2	3-0
2. 1st December 1962 (SC)	Manchester City A	H	8		1-0
3. 8th December 1962	Liverpool A	A	8		0-1
4. 15th December 1962 (SC)	Burnley A	H	8		4-2
5. 23rd March 1963	Burnley A	A	8	2	2-4
6. 6th April 1963	Preston North End A	H	7	1	8-2
7. 11th April 1963	Tranmere Rovers A	A	7		2-1
8. 13th April 1963	Blackpool A	A	7		1-1
9. 18th April 1963	Tranmere Rovers A	H	7	2	4-2
10. 27th April 1963	Liverpool A	H	11		6-4

B TEAM – LANCASHIRE LEAGUE DIVISION 2

			Shirt	Goals	Score
1. 18th August 1962 (SC)	Burnley B	H	8		0-2
2. 25th August 1962	Burnley B	A	8	1	2-5
3. 1st September 1962 (SC)	Manchester City B	A	8		6-0
4. 15th September 1962 (SC)	Burnley B	A	8	1	4-3
5. 29th September 1962 (SC)	Bury B	H	8		5-0
6. 6th October 1962 (SC)	Rochdale A	H	8	2	4-1
7. 13th October 1962	Bolton Wanderers B	A	8	2	3-1
8. 20th October 1962 (SC)	Rochdale A	A	8	1	1-1
9. 3rd November 1962	Bury B	H	8		2-1
10. 10th November 1962	Everton B	A	8		2-2
11. 26th December 1962	Blackburn Rovers B	H	8	1	1-0
12. 23rd February 1963	Oldham Athletic A	H	10		1-1
13. 2nd March 1963	Bury B	A	8	2	8-2
14. 9th March 1963	Manchester City B	A	8	4	7-0
15. 16th March 1963 (SC)	Bolton Wanderers B	H	7	2	3-0
16. 30th March 1963	Everton B	H	8	1	2-2
17. 2nd May 1963	Manchester City B	H	8	2	4-0
18. 21st May 1963	Oldham Athletic A	A	8		0-2

FA YOUTH CUP

			Shirt	Goals	Score
1. 24th April 1963 Round 4	Newcastle United	H	11		3-0
2. 30th April 1963 Round 5	Sheffield Wednesday	A	7		0-2

When George Best began the 1963 / 1964 season no one could possibly have anticipated the impact that he would have on the game of football. His campaign began on 24th August when he made his debut for the reserves in a home game against Sheffield Wednesday and helped the side to a 4-0 victory. On the 7th September George scored his first goal for the reserves in a home match against West Bromwich Albion. His performance brought his elevation to the first team the following against the same opponents at Old Trafford. United won the game 1-0 before Best returned to reserve and A team football. He scored for the reserves against Manchester City at home and Blackburn Rovers away and then netted seven goals in five appearances for the A team. Best added to his goals return by netting a hat trick in a FA Youth Cup 2nd round tie against Barrow at home. It was a game United won 14-1. This fine run of form led to George being recalled to first team action and he duly scored his first league goal against Burnley at Old Trafford 10 days later. A further first team goal followed when he netted against West Bromwich Albion away on 18th January. He scored FA Cup goals against Barnsley and Sunderland and he sandwiched a further two goals between the ties in the home league game against Bolton Wanderers on 19th February.

George had been a regular first team player since the turn of the year and his displays proved to be impressive. In April George returned to play in the FA Youth Cup and scored against Manchester City away in the Semi-final 2nd leg. He also scored in the 1st leg of the Final away to Swindon Town and finished with a winners' medal as Manchester United triumphed 5-2 on aggregate. It proved a magnificent first season for Best by playing impressively and scoring six first team goals in 26 appearances.

A TEAM – LANCASHIRE LEAGUE DIVISION 1

			Shirt	Goals	Score
1. 19th October 1963	Preston North End A	A	7	1	2-1
2. 26th October 1963	Rochdale Reserves	H	10		5-1
3. 2nd November 1963 (SC)	Manchester City A	H	7	1	2-3
4. 30th November 1963	Burnley A	A	7	3	6-2
5. 7th December 1963	Tranmere Rovers A	H	8	2	10-1

FA YOUTH CUP

			Shirt	Goals	Score
1. 18th December 1963 Round 2	Barrow	H	8	3	14-1
2. 8th April 1964 Semi-final 1st leg	Manchester City	H	8		4-1
3. 20th April 1964 Semi-final 2nd leg	Manchester City	A	8	1	4-3
4. 27th April 1964 Final 1st leg	Swindon Town	A	8	1	1-1
5. 30th April 1964 Final 2nd leg	Swindon Town	H	8		4-1

RESERVES – CENTRAL LEAGUE

			Shirt	Goals	Score
1. 24th August 1963	Sheffield Wednesday	H	11		4-0
2. 26th August 1963	Chesterfield	A	11		1-1
3. 7th September 1963	West Bromwich Albion	H	7	1	1-1
4. 9th September 1963	Blackpool	A	11		2-0
5. 21st September 1963	Huddersfield Town	H	7		3-1
6. 2nd October 1963	Manchester City	H	7	1	2-2
7. 12th October 1963	Blackburn Rovers	A	11	1	1-1
8. 9th November 1963	Aston Villa	A	7		1-2

LEAGUE DIVISION 1

			Shirt	Goals	Score
1. 14th September 1963	West Bromwich Albion	H	7		1-0
2. 28th December 1963	Burnley	H	11	1	5-1
3. 11th January 1964	Birmingham City	H	11		1-2
4. 18th January 1964	West Bromwich Albion	A	11	1	4-1
5. 1st February 1964	Arsenal	H	11		3-1
6. 8th February 1964	Leicester City	A	11		2-3
7. 19th February 1964	Bolton Wanderers	H	11	2	5-0
8. 22nd February 1964	Blackburn Rovers	A	11		3-1
9. 21st March 1964	Tottenham Hotspur	A	7		3-2
10. 23rd March 1964	Chelsea	H	7		1-1
11. 27th March 1964	Fulham	A	7		2-2
12. 28th March 1964	Wolverhampton Wanderers	H	7		2-2
13. 4th April 1964	Liverpool	A	7		0-3
14. 6th April 1964	Aston Villa	H	7		1-0
15. 13th April 1964	Sheffield United	H	7		2-1
16. 18th April 1964	Stoke City	A	7		1-3
17. 25th April 1964	Nottingham Forest	H	7		3-1

EUROPEAN CUP WINNERS' CUP

			Shirt	Goals	Score
1. 26th February 1964 Quarter-final 1st leg	Sporting Lisbon	H	11		4-1
2. 18th March 1964 Quarter-final 2nd leg	Sporting Lisbon	A	11		0-5

Reserve debut versus Sheffield Wednesday, 24th August 1963.

First team debut versus West Bromwich Albion, 14th September 1963.

Opposite. FA Youth Cup Semi-final, 2nd leg versus Manchester City, 20th April 1964.

Opposite. FA Youth Cup, Final, 2nd leg versus Swindon Town, 30th April 1964.

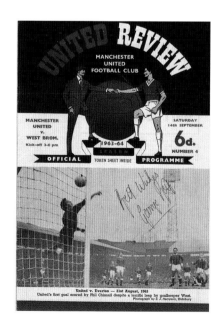

FA CUP						
			Shirt	**Goals**		**Score**
1. 4th January 1964 Round 3	Southampton	A	11			3-2
2. 25th January 1964 Round 4	Bristol Rovers	H	11			4-1
3. 15th February 1964 Round 5	Barnsley	A	11	1		4-0
4. 29th February 1964 Round 6	Sunderland	H	11	1		3-3
5. 4th March 1964 Round 6 Replay	Sunderland	A	11			2-2
6. 9th March 1964 Round 6 Second Replay	Sunderland	N	11			5-1
7. 14th March 1964 Semi-final	West Ham United	N	11			1-3

FRIENDLIES						
			Shirt	**Goals**		**Score**
1. 28th May 1964 Tour match	Bilbao XI	A	11			0-1

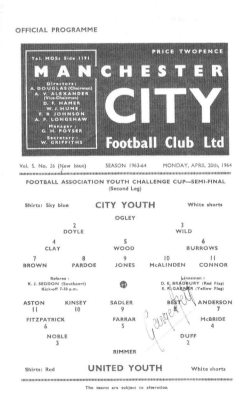

MANCHESTER UNITED YOUTH TEAM, 1963-64
Fitzpatrick, McBride, Farrar, Rimmer, Duff, Noble (Capt)
Anderson, Best, Sadler, Kinsey Aston.

The 1964 / 1965 season turned out to be George Best's first full campaign though it was one which began badly for United as they failed to win any of their first three games. Their first victory came on the 2nd September when Best scored in a 3-1 home win against West Ham United. Defeat at Fulham was followed by a draw at Everton before United won 12 of their next 13 league games. Best contributed goals against Everton, Chelsea and Blackburn Rovers plus others in the Inter-Cities Fairs Cup against Djurgaarden and Borussia Dortmund. By the end of November United headed the league by three points.

United lost 1-0 at home to Leeds United on 5th December which triggered a sequence in which the team managed to win only one of their next seven league games. The solitary victory came at Sheffield United on Boxing Day in which George scored the only goal. He scored a further goal against Chester in the 3rd round of the FA Cup and added to his tally by netting in a 3-2 home win against Burnley on 13th February.

Following a 1-0 defeat at Sunderland on 24th February, United won their next three games scoring 11 goals with George scoring against Chelsea in the 4-0 win on 13th March. He also scored in the previous game in the FA Cup 6th round 5-3 win at Wolverhampton Wanderers. Though defeated 1-0 at Sheffield Wednesday on 20th March, United won the next seven league games with Best contributing two goals in a 4-2 win at Birmingham City on 19th April and a one in a 3-1 home win against Arsenal on 26th April. Despite a 2-1 defeat at Aston Villa in the final league game of the season United became Division One Champions. Furthermore, they reached the Semi-finals of both the Inter-Cities Fairs and FA Cup competitions. George contributed fourteen goals to a successful campaign.

First goal of the season versus West Ham United, 2nd September 1964.

First away goal of the season versus Chelsea, 30th September 1964.

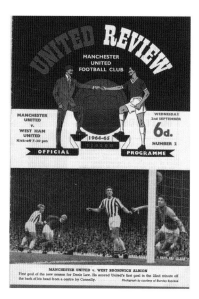

LEAGUE DIVISION 1

			Shirt	Goals	Score
1. 22nd August 1964	West Bromwich Albion	H	11		2-2
2. 24th August 1964	West Ham United	A	11		1-3
3. 29th August 1964	Leicester City	A	11		2-2
4. 2nd September 1964	West Ham United	H	11	1	3-1
5. 5th September 1964	Fulham	A	11		1-2
6. 8th September 1964	Everton	A	11		3-3
7. 12th September 1964	Nottingham Forest	H	11		3-0
8. 16th September 1964	Everton	H	11	1	2-1
9. 19th September 1964	Stoke City	A	11		2-1
10. 26th September 1964	Tottenham Hotspur	H	11		4-1
11. 30th September 1964	Chelsea	A	11	1	2-0
12. 6th October 1964	Burnley	A	11		0-0
13. 10th October 1964	Sunderland	H	11		1-0
14. 17th October 1964	Wolverhampton Wanderers	A	11		4-2
15. 24th October 1964	Aston Villa	H	11		7-0
16. 31st October 1964	Liverpool	A	11		2-0
17. 7th November 1964	Sheffield Wednesday	H	11		1-0
18. 21st November 1964	Blackburn Rovers	H	11	1	3-0
19. 28th November 1964	Arsenal	A	11		3-2
20. 5th December 1964	Leeds United	H	11		0-1
21. 12th December 1964	West Bromwich Albion	A	11		1-1
22. 16th December 1964	Birmingham City	H	11		1-1
23. 26th December 1964	Sheffield United	A	11	1	1-0
24. 28th December 1964	Sheffield United	H	11		1-1
25. 16th January 1965	Nottingham Forest	A	11		2-2
26. 23rd January 1965	Stoke City	H	11		1-1
27. 6th February 1965	Tottenham Hotspur	A	11		0-1
28. 13th February 1965	Burnley	H	11	1	3-2
29. 24th February 1965	Sunderland	A	11		0-1
30. 27th February 1965	Wolverhampton Wanderers	H	11		3-0
31. 13th March 1965	Chelsea	H	11	1	4-0
32. 15th March 1965	Fulham	H	11		4-1
33. 20th March 1965	Sheffield Wednesday	A	11		0-1
34. 22nd March 1965	Blackpool	H	11		2-0
35. 3rd April 1965	Blackburn Rovers	A	11		5-0
36. 12th April 1965	Leicester City	H	10		1-0
37. 17th April 1965	Leeds United	A	11		1-0
38. 19th April 1965	Birmingham City	A	11	2	4-2
39. 24th April 1965	Liverpool	H	11		3-0
40. 26th April 1965	Arsenal	H	11	1	3-1
41. 28th April 1965	Aston Villa	A	11		1-2

INTER-CITIES FAIRS CUP			Shirt	Goals	Score
1. 23rd September 1964 Round 1, 1st leg	Djurgaarden	A	11		1-1
2. 27th October 1964 Round 1, 2nd leg	Djurgaarden	H	11	1	6-1
3. 11th November 1964 Round 2, 1st leg	Borussia Dortmund	A	11	1	6-1
4. 2nd December 1964 Round 2, 2nd leg	Borussia Dortmund	H	11		4-0
5. 20th January 1965 Round 3, 1st leg	Everton	H	11		1-1
6. 9th February 1965 Round 3, 2nd leg	Everton	A	11		2-1
7. 12th May 1965 Quarter-final, 1st leg	Racing Strasbourg	A	11		5-0
8. 19th May 1965 Quarter-final, 2nd leg	Racing Strasbourg	H	11		0-0
9. 31st May 1965 Semi-final, 1st leg	Ferencvaros	H	11		3-2
10. 6th June 1965 Semi-final, 2nd leg	Ferencvaros	A	11		0-1
11. 16th June 1965 Semi-final Play-off	Ferencvaros	A	11		1-2

*Opposite. Two goals
versus Birmingham City,
19th April 1965.*

*Opposite. Final goal of
the season versus Arsenal,
26th April 1965.*

FA CUP					
			Shirt	Goals	Score
1. 9th January 1965 Round 3	Chester	H	11	1	2-1
2. 30th January 1965 Round 4	Stoke City	A	11		0-0
3. 3rd February 1965 Round 4 Replay	Stoke City	H	11		1-0
4. 20th February 1965 Round 5	Burnley	H	11		2-1
5. 10th March 1965 Round 6	Wolverhampton Wanderers	A	11	1	5-3
6. 27th March 1965 Semi-final	Leeds United	N	11		0-0
7. 31st March 1965 Semi-final Replay	Leeds United	N	11		0-1

FRIENDLIES					
			Shirt	Goals	Score
1. 12th August 1964	Hamburg	A	11		3-1
2. 14th August 1964	Shamrock Rovers	A	11	1	4-2

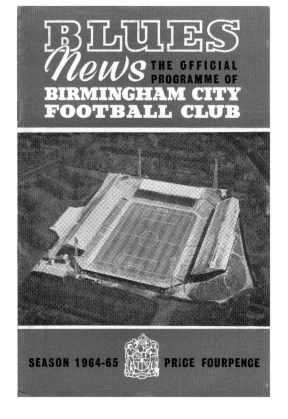

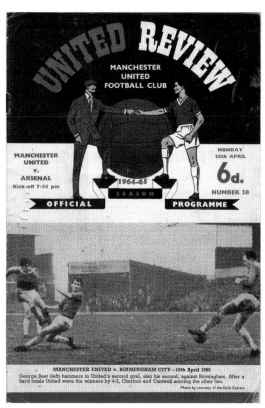

MANCHESTER UNITED v. BIRMINGHAM CITY—19th April 1965
George Best (left) hammers in United's second goal, also his second, against Birmingham. After a hard tussle United were the winners by 4-2, Charlton and Cantwell scoring the other two.
Photo by courtesy of the Daily Express

Manchester United began the season with a 1-0 home win against Sheffield Wednesday and then failed to win any of their next four league games. Best's first goal of the season came in a 4-2 away defeat at Nottingham Forest on 24th August although United's season continued to stutter. Best missed league games against Chelsea at home and Arsenal away but he returned to score twice in a 6-0 home rout against HJK Helsinki in the European Cup 1st round 2nd leg tie. George followed this three days with a goal against Liverpool in a 2-0 home win.

Despite a 5-1 thrashing at Tottenham Hotspur on 16th October, United began a 10 league game unbeaten run during which they won seven matches. Best scored in a emphatic 5-0 win at Leicester City and then scored two more a week later in a 3-1 home victory against Sheffield United. He followed this up with two more goals in a 3-2 win at Sunderland and a solitary strike against Everton at Old Trafford. Another poor run saw United fail to win their next three league games at the beginning of 1966 though George managed to score in a 1-1 home draw against Sunderland on 8th January. He netted another double in the 3rd round FA Cup tie against Derby County on 22nd January as United team triumphed 5-2.

Best failed to score in any of his last nine league appearances for United in 1965 / 1966 though he did score in the FA Cup 5th round tie at Wolverhampton Wanderers on 5th March in which United triumphed 4-2. Four days later United, and George in particular, played in one of their finest ever games when they defeated Benfica away in the European Cup Quarter-final 2nd leg. George scored twice in the opening twelve minutes as United ran out 5-1 winners. Sadly, fortunes changed for George as he limped out of the European Cup Semi-final 1st leg tie at FK Partizan Belgrade on 13th April as United lost the game 2-0. His injury required cartilage surgery and his season was ended prematurely.

During Best's absence, United managed to win just three of their last eight league games and finished the season in a disappointing fourth place. Additionally, they failed to pull back a two goal deficit in the European Cup Semi-final 2nd leg. United won the return game against FK Partizan Belgrade 1-0 at Old Trafford but it wasn't enough. The team reached the Semi-final of the FA Cup too but were defeated 1-0 by Everton. Best contributed sixteen goals to United's campaign and it might have more had not injury intervened at a vital stage of the team's season.

Opposite. Goal versus Everton, 15th December 1965,

Opposite. Goal versus Sunderland, 8th January 1966.

Opposite. Two goals versus Derby County (FA Cup, Round 3), 22nd January 1966.

Opposite. Two goals versus Benfica (European Cup Quarter-final, 2nd leg), 9th March 1966.

LEAGUE DIVISION 1

			Shirt	Goals	Score
1. 21st August 1965	Sheffield Wednesday	H	10		1-0
2. 24th August 1965	Nottingham Forest	A	10	1	2-4
3. 28th August 1965	Northampton Town	A	11		1-1
4. 1st September 1965	Nottingham Forest	H	11		0-0
5. 4th September 1965	Stoke City	H	11		1-1
6. 8th September 1965	Newcastle United	A	11		2-1
7. 11th September 1965	Burnley	A	11		0-3
8. 15th September 1965	Newcastle United	H	11		1-1
9. 9th October 1965	Liverpool	H	8	1	2-0
10. 16th October 1965	Tottenham Hotspur	A	8		1-5
11. 23rd October 1965	Fulham	H	8		4-1
12. 30th October 1965	Blackpool	A	8		2-1
13. 6th November 1965	Blackburn Rovers	H	7		2-2
14. 13th November 1965	Leicester City	A	7	1	5-0
15. 20th November 1965	Sheffield United	H	7	2	3-1
16. 4th December 1965	West Ham United	H	7		0-0
17. 11th December 1965	Sunderland	A	7	2	3-2
18. 15th December 1965	Everton	H	7	1	3-0
19. 18th December 1965	Tottenham Hotspur	H	7		5-1
20. 27th December 1965	West Bromwich Albion	H	7		1-1
21. 1st January 1966	Liverpool	A	7		1-2
22. 8th January 1966	Sunderland	H	7	1	1-1
23. 12th January 1966	Leeds United	A	7		1-1
24. 15th January 1966	Fulham	A	7		1-0
25. 29th January 1966	Sheffield Wednesday	A	7		0-0
26. 5th February 1966	Northampton Town	H	7		6-2
27. 19th February 1966	Stoke City	A	8		2-2
29. 26th February 1966	Burnley	H	7		4-2
29. 12th March 1966	Chelsea	A	7		0-2
30. 19th March 1966	Arsenal	H	7		2-1
31. 9th April 1966	Leicester City	H	7		1-2

FRIENDLIES

			Shirt	Goals	Score
1. 8th August 1965	Hanover	A	11		0-2
2. 10th August 1965	Nuremburg	A	11		0-2

EUROPEAN CUP

			Shirt	Goals	Score
1. 6th October 1965 Preliminary Round 2nd leg	HJK Helsinki	H	8	2	6-0
2. 17th November 1965 Round 1, 1st leg	ASK Vorwaerts	A	7		2-0
3. 1st December 1965 Round 1, 2nd leg	ASK Vorwaerts	H	7		3-1
4. 2nd February 1966 Quarter-final, 1st leg	Benfica	H	7		3-2
5. 9th March 1966 Quarter-final, 2nd leg	Benfica	A	7	2	5-1
6. 13th April 1966 Semi final, 1st leg	FK Partizan Belgrade	A	7		0-2

FA CUP

			Shirt	Goals	Score
1. 22nd January 1966 Round 3	Derby County	A	7	2	5-2
2. 12th February 1966 Round 4	Rotherham United	H	7		0-0
3. 15th February 1966 Round 4 Replay	Rotherham United	A	7		1-0
4. 5th March 1966 Round 5	Wolverhampton Wanderers	A	7	1	4-2
5. 26th March 1966 Round 6	Preston North End	A	7		1-1

FA CHARITY SHIELD

			Shirt	Goals	Score
1. 14th August 1965	Liverpool	H	7	1	2-2

Best played in all 42 league games in the 1966 / 1967 season and was the only United ever present. He scored in the opening game of the season as the team beat West Bromwich Albion 5-3 at Old Trafford. Best scored again in United's third match in a 3-1 defeat at Leeds United before he hit a lean spell. He went 10 league games without scoring until he netted in a 3-1 win at Chelsea on 5th November. United proceeded to win the next four games with George scoring in a 2-1 victory at Leicester City. Despite a 2-1 defeat at Aston Villa on 3rd December United were well in contention to win their fifth league title since the war. Best scored both goals in a 2-2 home draw against Liverpool the week after.

United entered a mixed spell prior to Christmas and into the New Year while George lost his scoring touch during the same period. The team won three out of seven league games, drawing three and losing at Sheffield United on Boxing Day. Best went 15 league and FA Cup games without scoring though by the time he rediscovered his goal touch in a 2-2 at Fulham on 27th March United were on course to win the league title. He scored again in a 3-0 home win against West Ham United five days later. United won three out of their next five league games with Best scoring in successive wins against Aston Villa and West Ham United. It was in the latter of these matches that United clinched their seventh Championship title as they routed The Hammers 6-1 at Upton Park in the penultimate game of the season.

The campaign had proved a successful one for United. Despite early exits in both the League and FA Cup competitions they secured the league title four points ahead of Nottingham Forest. George had again played a key part by scoring ten league goals.

FRIENDLIES			Shirt	Goals	Score
1. 6th August 1966	Celtic	A	7		1-4
2. 10th August 1966	Bayern Munich	A	7		1-4
3. 12th August 1966	FK Austria	A	11		2-5
4. 12th October 1966 British week celebrations	Fiorentina	A	11	1	2-1
5. 17th May 1967 American Tour match	Benfica	N	8		1-3
6. 23rd May 1967 American Tour match	Dundee	N	7		2-4
7. 28th May 1967 New Zealand Tour match	Auckland	A	7	1	8-1
8. 31st May 1967 New Zealand Tour match	New Zealand	A	7	2	11-0
9. 4th June 1967 Australian Tour match	Queensland	A	7	2	7-0
10. 7th June 1967 Australian Tour match	Representative XI	A	7	2	3-0
11. 11th June 1967 Australian Tour match	Victoria XI	A	7		1-1
12. 12th June 1967 Australian Tour match	Northern NSW	A	7	1	3-0
13. 18th June 1967 Australian Tour match	New South Wales	A	7		3-1
14. 21st June 1967 Australian Tour match	Victoria State XI	A	7	1	4-0
15. 24th June 1967 Australian Tour match	South Australia	A	7		5-1
16. 27th June 1967 Australian Tour match	Western Australia	A	7	3	7-0

LEAGUE DIVISION 1			Shirt	Goals	Score
1. 20th August 1966	West Bromwich Albion	H	7	1	5-3
2. 23rd August 1966	Everton	A	7		2-1
3. 27th August 1966	Leeds United	A	7	1	1-3
4. 31st August 1966	Everton	H	11		3-0
5. 3rd September 1966	Newcastle United	H	11		3-2
6. 7th September 1966	Stoke City	A	11		0-3
7. 10th September 1966	Tottenham Hotspur	A	7		1-2
8. 17th September 1966	Manchester City	H	7		1-0
9. 24th September 1966	Burnley	H	11		4-1
10. 1st October 1966	Nottingham Forest	A	7		1-4
11. 8th October 1966	Blackpool	A	11		2-1
12. 15th October 1966	Chelsea	H	11		1-1
13. 29th October 1966	Arsenal	H	11		1-0
14. 5th November 1966	Chelsea	A	11	1	3-1
15. 12th November 1966	Sheffield Wednesday	H	11		2-0
16. 19th November 1966	Southampton	A	11		2-1
17. 26th November 1966	Sunderland	H	7		5-0
18. 30th November 1966	Leicester City	A	7	1	2-1
19. 3rd December 1966	Aston Villa	A	7		1-2
20. 10th December 1966	Liverpool	H	7	2	2-2
21. 17th December 1966	West Bromwich Albion	A	7		4-3
22. 26th December 1966	Sheffield United	A	7		1-2
23. 27th December 1966	Sheffield United	H	7		2-0
24. 31st December 1966	Leeds United	H	7		0-0
25. 14th January 1967	Tottenham Hotspur	H	7		1-0
26. 21st January 1967	Manchester City	A	11		1-1
27. 4th February 1967	Burnley	A	7		1-1
28. 11th February 1967	Nottingham Forest	H	7		1-0
29. 25th February 1967	Blackpool	H	7		4-0
30. 3rd March 1967	Arsenal	A	7		1-1
31. 11th March 1967	Newcastle United	A	7		0-0
32. 18th March 1967	Leicester City	H	7		5-2
33. 25th March 1967	Liverpool	A	7		0-0
34. 27th March 1967	Fulham	A	7	1	2-2
35. 28th March 1967	Fulham	H	7		2-1
36. 1st April 1967	West Ham United	H	7	1	3-0
37. 10th April 1967	Sheffield Wednesday	A	7		2-2
38. 18th April 1967	Southampton	H	7		3-0
39. 22nd April 1967	Sunderland	A	7		0-0
40. 29th April 1967	Aston Villa	H	7	1	3-1
41. 6th May 1967	West Ham United	A	7	1	6-1
42. 13th May 1967	Stoke City	H	7		0-0

FA CUP			Shirt	Goals	Score
1. 28th January 1967 Round 3	Stoke City	H	7		2-0
2. 18th February 1967 Round 4	Norwich City	H	11		1-2

LEAGUE CUP			Shirt	Goals	Score
1. 14th September 1966 Round 2	Blackpool	A	8		1-5

First goal of the season versus Leeds United, 27th August 1966.

Two goals versus Liverpool, 10th December 1966.

Goal versus Aston Villa, 29th April 1967.

Goal versus West Ham United, 6th May 1967.

This season began inconsistently for both United and Best. The team were beaten 3-1 away at Everton in the first game while George missed the second match as United beat Leeds United 1-0 at Old Trafford. United drew 1-1 at home to Leicester City and followed this with a 3-1 victory at West Ham United. Three consecutive draws came next with George scoring his first goal of the season in the last of these games at Sheffield Wednesday on 16th September. He followed this up with two more goals the following week in the 3-1 home win against Tottenham Hotspur. Four consecutive league victories followed with Best netting against Coventry City at Old Trafford on 25th October in a 4-0 victory. He scored a further goal at Nottingham Forest three days later though United lost 3-1.

A 2-1 victory for United at Liverpool on 11th November saw Best score both goals. He opened his goal scoring account in the European Cup on 29th November when he scored against FK Sarajevo in a 2-1 win in the 2nd round 2nd leg at Old Trafford. George found the back of the net twice at West Bromwich Albion on 2nd December in a 2-1 win and then scored two more in the 4-0 home win against Wolverhampton Wanderers on Boxing Day. At the turn of the year Best hit a rich vein of scoring form when he netted in the next six matches managing a goal against West Ham United, two against Sheffield Wednesday, one against Tottenham Hotspur in the 3rd round of the FA Cup at Old Trafford. He scored solitary goals in league games against Tottenham Hotspur, Burnley and Arsenal.

United's form stalled a little in March as they lost three of their next five league games. They also lost 1-0 in their European Cup Quarter-final 2nd leg tie against Gornik Zabrze though progressed 2-1 on aggregate. Best scored in a 3-1 home defeat to Manchester City on 27th March and again three days later in a 4-2 victory at Stoke City. His fine goal scoring form continued into April as he netted against Liverpool, Fulham (home and away) and Southampton. Importantly, Best scored the only goal in the European Cup Semi-final 1st leg at Old Trafford on 24th April. United progressed to the final after drawing 3-3 in the return leg against Real Madrid.

On 4th May Best scored a hat-trick as United routed Newcastle United 6-0 at Old Trafford and scored again seven days later against Sunderland at home. Unfortunately, United lost the game 2-1 and so conceded the Championship title to Manchester City. The season though ended on a high note for both Best and his club after United beat Benfica 4-1 at Wembley Stadium to secure the European Cup with George scoring the second goal. It proved a great campaign for both United and Best as he finished the team's top goal scorer with 28 league goals and four more in the Domestic and European competitions. His achievements were recognised when he was named British Footballer of the Year.

LEAGUE DIVISION 1

			Shirt	Goals	Score
1. 19th August 1967	Everton	A	7		1-3
2. 26th August 1967	Leicester City	H	7		1-1
3. 2nd September 1967	West Ham United	A	11		3-1
4. 6th September 1967	Sunderland	A	11		1-1
5. 9th September 1967	Burnley	H	11		2-2
6. 16th September 1967	Sheffield Wednesday	A	7	1	1-1
7. 23rd September 1967	Tottenham Hotspur	H	7	2	3-1
8. 30th September 1967	Manchester City	A	7		2-1
9. 7th October 1967	Arsenal	H	7		1-0
10. 14th October 1967	Sheffield United	A	7		3-0
11. 25th October 1967	Coventry City	H	7	1	4-0
12. 28th October 1967	Nottingham Forest	A	7	1	1-3
13. 4th November 1967	Stoke City	H	10		1-0
14. 8th November 1967	Leeds United	A	10		0-1
15. 11th November 1967	Liverpool	A	10	2	2-1
16. 18th November 1967	Southampton	H	10		3-2
17. 25th November 1967	Chelsea	A	10		1-1
18. 2nd December 1967	West Bromwich Albion	H	10	2	2-1
19. 9th December 1967	Newcastle United	A	10		2-2
20. 16th December 1967	Everton	H	7		3-1
21. 23rd December 1967	Leicester City	A	7		2-2
22. 26th December 1967	Wolverhampton Wanderers	H	7	2	4-0
23. 30th December 1967	Wolverhampton Wanderers	A	7		3-2
24. 6th January 1968	West Ham United	H	7	1	3-1
25. 20th January 1968	Sheffield Wednesday	H	7	2	4-2
26. 3rd February 1968	Tottenham Hotspur	A	7	1	2-1
27. 17th February 1968	Burnley	A	7	1	1-2
28. 24th February 1968	Arsenal	A	7	1	2-0
29. 2nd March 1968	Chelsea	H	7		1-3
30. 16th March 1968	Coventry City	A	7		0-2
31. 23rd March 1968	Nottingham Forest	H	10		3-0
32. 27th March 1968	Manchester City	H	10	1	1-3
33. 30th March 1968	Stoke City	A	7	1	4-2
34. 6th April 1968	Liverpool	H	7	1	1-2
35. 12th April 1968	Fulham	A	7	2	4-0
36. 13th April 1968	Southampton	A	7	1	2-2
37. 15th April 1968	Fulham	H	7	1	3-0
38. 20th April 1968	Sheffield United	H	7		1-0
39. 27th April 1968	West Bromwich Albion	A	7		3-6
40. 4th May 1968	Newcastle United	H	7	3	6-0
41. 11th May 1968	Sunderland	H	7	1	1-2

EUROPEAN CUP				Shirt	Goals	Score
1. 20th September 1967 Round 1, 1st leg	Hibernians (Malta)	H		7		4-0
2. 27th September 1967 Round 1, 2nd leg	Hibernians (Malta)	A		7		0-0
3. 15th November 1967 Round 2, 1st leg	FK Sarajevo	A		10		0-0
4. 29th November 1967 Round 2, 2nd leg	FK Sarajevo	H		10	1	2-1
5. 28th February 1968 Quarter-final, 1st leg	Gornik Zabrze	H		7		2-0
6. 13th March 1968 Quarter-final, 2nd leg	Gornik Zabrze	A		11		0-1
7. 24th April 1968 Semi-final, 1st leg	Real Madrid	H		7	1	1-0
8. 15th May 1968 Semi-final, 2nd leg	Real Madrid	A		7		3-3
9. 29th May 1968 Final	Benfica	N		7	1	4-1

Two goals versus Fulham, 12th April 1968.

Goal versus Real Madrid (European Cup, Semi-final, 1st leg), 24th April 1968.

Opposite. Hat-trick versus Newcastle United, 4th May 1968.

Opposite. Goal versus Benfica (European Cup final), 29th May 1968.

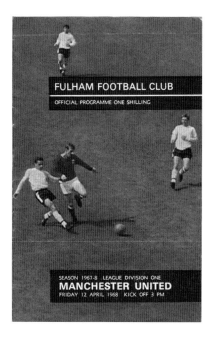

FA CUP

			Shirt	Goals	Score
1. 27th January 1968 Round 3	Tottenham Hotspur	H	7	1	2-2
2. 31st January 1968 Round 3 Replay	Tottenham Hotspur	A	7		0-1

FA CHARITY SHIELD

			Shirt	Goals	Score
1. 12th August 1967	Tottenham Hotspur	H	7		3-3

FRIENDLIES

			Shirt	Goals	Score
1. 15th August 1967	Italian Olympic XI	H	7		2-0

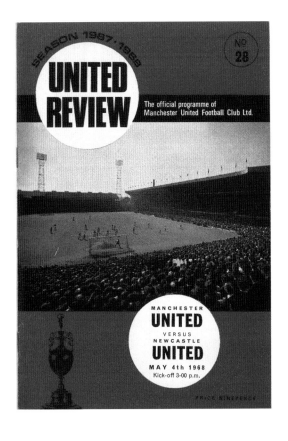

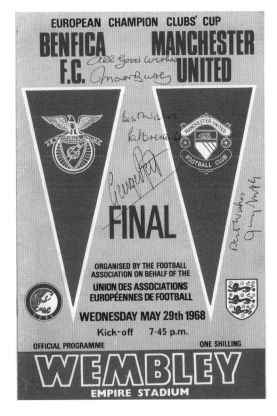

The season started well for United and Best. He scored in the first game of the season in a 2-1 home win against Everton. Unfortunately, he then failed to score in any of the next five league games until he netted at Sheffield Wednesday on 31st August in a thrilling game which United lost 5-4. He followed this up on 21st September with two goals against Newcastle United at Old Trafford as United won 3-1. The team's form proved rather erratic as they failed to win any of their next three league games. Best though did score in a 2-1 home defeat against Southampton on 19th October. Three days previously the Irishman was sent off for the first time in his career. He was given his marching orders against Estudiantes at home in the 2nd leg of the World Club Championship. It was a game United drew 1-1 though they lost the tie 2-1 on aggregate.

Best netted two goals in a 3-2 home win against Queens Park Rangers on 26th October while his side then drew four consecutive league games with three of them finishing goalless. The run of stalemates ended on 30th November when George scored in a 2-0 home win against Wolverhampton Wanderers at Old Trafford. United's inconsistent form continued as they managed to win only one of their next five league games. Best rediscovered his goal scoring touch on 18th January by netting once as United beat Sunderland 4-1 at home. Another poor run saw United fail to win any of their next five league games though George did manage to score in the 2-2 at Wolverhampton Wanderers on 15th February. He had also converted at Birmingham City the week before in the FA Cup 5th round tie which had ended 2-2. On the 26th of the month he also scored two more goals against Rapid Vienna in the European Cup Quarter-final 1st leg tie which United won 3-0 at Old Trafford.

Manchester United recorded their best win of the season on 19th March when they ran out 8-1 winners against Queens Park Rangers at home with Best adding two more goals to his tally. He then scored another goal in the next home league game against Sheffield Wednesday three days later. Two draws followed against Stoke City and West Ham United before George scored the only goal of the game in a win at Nottingham Forest on 31st March. He then converted two more in the next game against West Bromwich Albion at home on 2nd April which United won 2-1 and then contributed a solitary goal three days later at Old Trafford as his side beat Nottingham Forest 3-1.

Defeats at Coventry City and Newcastle United followed before United finished their league season with two home wins against Burnley on 19th April and Leicester City on 17th May. While George contributed a goal in each of the matches the season for United had been a disappointment. They finished 11th in the league and were eliminated from the FA Cup at the Quarter-final stage. Bigger frustration followed in the European Cup as United narrowly lost 2-1 on aggregate to AC Milan in the Semi-finals. On a personal level though, George was presented with the European Footballer of the Year Trophy in a season which he netted 22 goals in all competitions.

LEAGUE DIVISION 1

			Shirt	Goals	Score
1. 10th August 1968	Everton	H	7	1	2-1
2. 14th August 1968	West Bromwich Albion	A	7		1-3
3. 17th August 1968	Manchester City	A	7		0-0
4. 21st August 1968	Coventry City	H	11		1-0
5. 24th August 1968	Chelsea	H	11		0-4
6. 28th August 1968	Tottenham Hotspur	H	11		3-1
7. 31st August 1968	Sheffield Wednesday	A	11	1	4-5
8. 7th September 1968	West Ham United	H	11		1-1
9. 14th September 1968	Burnley	A	11		0-1
10. 21st September 1968	Newcastle United	H	11	2	3-1
11. 5th October 1968	Arsenal	H	11		0-0
12. 9th October 1968	Tottenham Hotspur	A	11		2-2
13. 19th October 1968	Southampton	H	11	1	1-2
14. 26th October 1968	Queens Park Rangers	A	11	2	3-2
15. 2nd November 1968	Leeds United	H	11		0-0
16. 9th November 1968	Sunderland	A	11		1-1
17. 16th November 1968	Ipswich Town	H	11		0-0
18. 23rd November 1968	Stoke City	A	8		0-0
19. 30th November 1968	Wolverhampton Wanderers	H	11	1	2-0
20. 7th December 1968	Leicester City	A	11		1-2
21. 14th December 1968	Liverpool	H	7		1-0
22. 21st December 1968	Southampton	A	7		0-2
23. 26th December 1968	Arsenal	A	7		0-3
24. 11th January 1969	Leeds United	A	7		1-2
25. 18th January 1969	Sunderland	H	11	1	4-1
26. 1st February 1969	Ipswich Town	A	11		0-1
27. 15th February 1969	Wolverhampton Wanderers	A	11	1	2-2
28. 8th March 1969	Manchester City	H	11		0-1
29. 10th March 1969	Everton	A	7		0-0
30. 15th March 1969	Chelsea	A	11		2-3
31. 19th March 1969	Queens Park Rangers	H	11	2	8-1
32. 22nd March 1969	Sheffield Wednesday	H	9	1	1-0
33. 24th March 1969	Stoke City	H	11		1-1
34. 29th March 1969	West Ham United	A	11		0-0
35. 31st March 1969	Nottingham Forest	A	11	1	1-0
36. 2nd April 1969	West Bromwich Albion	H	11	2	2-1
37. 5th April 1969	Nottingham Forest	H	11	1	3-1
38. 8th April 1969	Coventry City	A	11		1-2
39. 12th April 1969	Newcastle United	A	11		0-2
40. 19th April 1969	Burnley	H	11	1	2-0
41. 17th May 1969	Leicester City	H	11	1	3-2

EUROPEAN CUP

			Shirt	Goals	Score
1. 18th September 1968 Round 1, 1st leg	Waterford	A	7		3-1
2. 2nd October 1968 Round 1, 2nd leg	Waterford	H	7		7-1
3. 26th February 1969 Quarter-final, 1st leg	Rapid Vienna	H	11	2	3-0
4. 5th March 1969 Quarter-final, 2nd leg	Rapid Vienna	A	11		0-0
5. 23rd April 1969 Semi-final, 1st leg	AC Milan	A	11		0-2
6. 15th May 1969 Semi-final, 2nd leg	AC Milan	H	11		1-0

WORLD CLUB CHAMPIONSHIP

			Shirt	Goals	Score
1. 25th September 1968 1st leg	Estudiantes	A	11		0-1
2. 16th October 1968 2nd leg	Estudiantes	H	11		1-1

FRIENDLIES

			Shirt	Goals	Score
1. 31st July 1968	Hamburg SV	A	7	1	2-0
2. 4th August 1968	Drumcondra Select	A	7		2-1

FA CUP			Shirt	Goals	Score
1. 4th January 1969 Round 3	Exeter City	A	7		3-1
2. 25th January 1969 Round 4	Watford	H	8		1-1
3. 3rd February 1969 Round 4 Replay	Watford	A	11		2-0
4. 8th February 1969 Round 5	Birmingham City	A	11	1	2-2
5. 24th February 1969 Round 5 Replay	Birmingham City	H	11		6-2
6. 1st March 1969 Round 6	Everton	A	11		0-1

Goal versus Everton, 10th August 1968.

Sent off versus Estudiantes (World Club Championship, 2nd leg), 16th October 1968.

Two goals versus Rapid Vienna (European Cup, Quarter-final, 1st leg), 26th February 1969.

Two goals versus Queens Park Rangers, 19th March 1969.

The season began with managerial changes which saw Sir Matt Busby elevated to General Manager while Wilf McGuinness became Chief Coach responsible for team selection. The changes had a disastrous effect on early season form as United failed to win any of their opening six league games. Best helped to kick start the campaign with a goal in a 3-1 home win against Sunderland on 30th August and then netted both goals the following week in a 2-2 draw at Leeds United.

United's form continued to improve as the team lost just one of their next eight league games with George contributing the same number of goals during this run. Following a 2-0 defeat at Derby County on 4th October, Best scored in three consecutive league games away at Southampton and at home to Ipswich Town and Nottingham Forest. He had also prospered in the League Cup by scoring in home ties against Wrexham and Burnley. His next league goal was also scored against Burnley at Turf Moor in a 1-1 draw on 29th November. Four days later at the end of the League Cup Semi-final 1st leg tie at Manchester City Best knocked the match ball from the hands of the referee. It was a game United lost 2-1 but Best's actions resulted in him being fined £100 and suspended for four weeks.

George returned from his ban to play in the FA Cup 5th Round tie at Northampton Town on 7th February. His play proved scintillating as he scored six times as United won the game 8-2. United managed to win just one of their next seven league games with Best scoring once in a 3-3 home draw against Burnley. United's form improved as they won two of their last four league matches. Best scored in the 7-0 home rout against West Bromwich Albion on 8th April He then netted in the last game of the season as United drew 2-2 with Sheffield Wednesday at Old Trafford.

Manchester United finished the league season in eighth place and reached the Semi-finals of both the League Cup and FA Cup competitions. Best's suspension apart, it proved another good season for George as he finished the team's top goal scorer for the third season in succession, netting 15 league goals and a further eight in the two domestic cup competitions.

Goal versus Sunderland, 30th August 1969.

Goal versus Burnley, 29th November 1969.

LEAGUE DIVISION 1			Shirt	Goals	Score
1. 9th August 1969	Crystal Palace	A	11		2-2
2. 13th August 1969	Everton	H	11		0-2
3. 16th August 1969	Southampton	H	11		1-4
4. 19th August 1969	Everton	A	10		0-3
5. 23rd August 1969	Wolverhampton Wanderers	A	11		0-0
6. 27th August 1969	Newcastle United	H	11		0-0
7. 30th August 1969	Sunderland	H	11	1	3-1
8. 6th September 1969	Leeds United	A	11	2	2-2
9. 13th September 1969	Liverpool	H	11		1-0
10. 17th September 1969	Sheffield Wednesday	A	11	2	3-1
11. 20th September 1969	Arsenal	A	11	1	2-2
12. 27th September 1969	West Ham United	H	11	2	5-2
13. 4th October 1969	Derby County	A	11		0-2
14. 8th October 1969	Southampton	A	11	1	3-0
15. 11th October 1969	Ipswich Town	H	11	1	2-1
16. 18th October 1969	Nottingham Forest	H	11	1	1-1
17. 25th October 1969	West Bromwich Albion	A	11		1-2
18. 1st November 1969	Stoke City	H	11		1-1
19. 8th November 1969	Coventry City	A	8		2-1
20. 15th November 1969	Manchester City	A	8		0-4
21. 22nd November 1969	Tottenham Hotspur	H	10		3-1
22. 29th November 1969	Burnley	A	7	1	1-1
23. 6th December 1969	Chelsea	H	7		0-2
24. 13th December 1969	Liverpool	A	8		4-1
25. 26th December 1969	Wolverhampton Wanderers	H	11		0-0
26. 27th December 1969	Sunderland	A	11		1-1
27. 10th February 1970	Ipswich Town	A	11		1-0
28. 14th February 1970	Crystal Palace	H	11		1-1
29. 28th February 1970	Stoke City	A	11		2-2
30. 17th March 1970	Burnley	H	11	1	3-3
31. 21st March 1970	Chelsea	A	11		1-2
32. 28th March 1970	Manchester City	H	11		1-2
33. 30th March 1970	Coventry City	H	8		1-1
34. 31st March 1970	Nottingham Forest	A	11		2-1
35. 8th April 1970	West Bromwich Albion	H	11	1	7-0
36. 13th April 1970	Tottenham Hotspur	A	11		1-2
37. 15th April 1970	Sheffield Wednesday	H	11	1	2-2

FA CUP

			Shirt	Goals	Score
1. 3rd January 1970 Round 3	Ipswich Town	A	11		1-0
2. 7th February 1970 Round 5	Northampton Town	A	11	6	8-2
3. 21st February 1970 Round 6	Middlesbrough	A	11		1-1
4. 25th February 1970 Round 6 Replay	Middlesbrough	H	11		2-1
5. 14th March 1970 Semi-final	Leeds United	N	11		0-0
6. 23rd March 1970 Semi-final, Replay	Leeds United	N	11		0-0
7. 26th March 1970 Semi-final, Second Replay	Leeds United	N	11		0-1
8. 10th April 1970 Third-place Play-off	Watford	N	11		2-0

LEAGUE CUP

			Shirt	Goals	Score
1. 3rd September 1969 Round 2	Middlesbrough	H	11		1-0
2. 23rd September 1969 Round 3	Wrexham	H	11	1	2-0
3. 14th October 1969 Round 4	Burnley	A	11		0-0
4. 20th October 1969 Round 4, Replay	Burnley	H	11	1	1-0
5. 12th November 1969 Round 5	Derby County	A	8		0-0
6. 19th November 1969 Round 5, Replay	Derby County	H	7		1-0
7. 3rd December 1969 Semi-final, 1st leg	Manchester City	A	7		1-2
8. 17th December 1969 Semi-final, 2nd leg	Manchester City	H	11		2-2

FRIENDLIES			Shirt	Goals	Score
1. 26th July 1969 Prince of Wales Investiture match	Welsh XI	A	11		2-0
2. 31st July 1969	Copenhagen Select	A	11	1	6-2
3. 2nd August 1969	FC Zurich	A	11	1	9-1
4. 26th April 1969	Bermuda XI	A	Sub		4-2
5. 30th April 1970 Bermuda Tour match	Bermuda Football Union	N	9	2	6-1
6. 2nd May 1970 Canada Tour Match	Bari	N	11		1-0
7. 5th May 1970 America Tour Match	Bari	N	11	1	2-1
8. 11th May 1970 Canada Tour Match	Celtic	N	11		2-0
9. 13th May 1970 America Tour match	Eintracht Frankfurt	N	10	1	2-1
10. 17th May 1970 America Tour match	Eintracht Frankfurt	N	11	1	2-3

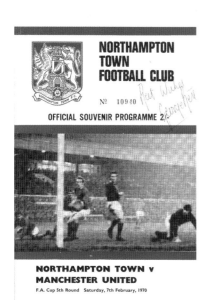

Six goals versus Northampton Town (FA Cup, Round 5), 7th February 1970.

Goal versus Sheffield Wednesday, 15th April 1970.

Manchester United began the new season poorly by losing two of their first three games. Best did not manage to score until the sixth league game when he netted on the 2nd September in a 2-0 home win against Everton. The following week he scored in the 2nd round League Cup 3-1 win at Aldershot. Best netted again on 12th September in a 2-0 home win against Coventry City though this was followed by a 4-0 defeat at Ipswich Town which left United 12th in the league. While Best scored in the next game against Blackpool in a 1-1 home draw United managed to win just one of their next six league games with George failing to find the net.

George scored in a 2-1 win against Chelsea in the League Cup 4th round tie at Old Trafford on 28th October and then converted in consecutive league draws against Huddersfield Town at home and Tottenham Hotspur away. United were then defeated at home to Manchester City 4-1 and then Arsenal beat them 3-1 at Old Trafford. The next game saw George score in a 4-4 draw against Derby County on Boxing Day though by early January United were languishing in fifteenth place. Meanwhile, Best had appeared before an FA disciplinary commission after acquiring three cautions for misconduct in a twelve month period. He had arrived three hours late was fined £250 and given a six week suspended sentence. The next day Best scored in the FA Cup 5th round replay at Middlesbrough though United lost 2-1 Three days later Best missed the train taking the United team to their league game at Chelsea. He took a later train to London though decided to spend the weekend with actress Sinead Cusack instead. Best was suspended for two weeks by the Club and he missed the home game against Burnley on 16th January. He was though allowed to play for a Rangers / Celtic select team at Hampden Park on 27th January in a benefit game to help the dependants of the victims of the Ibrox disaster. Best scored but his side lost 2-1 to a Scotland XI.

George returned to first team action on 30th January in a 2-1 away win at Huddersfield Town. He returned to scoring form on 6th February in a 2-1 home victory against Tottenham Hotspur. Despite a 4-3 defeat at West Bromwich Albion on 6th March Best scored in this and the next three consecutive league games against Nottingham Forest, Stoke City (two) and West Ham United. George managed a further goal at Coventry City on 13th April and followed this with two more in the 5-3 win against Crystal Palace four days later. United were unbeaten in their last three games of the season in which Best scored against Ipswich Town at home on 24th April. He added two more in the final game of the season as United triumphed 4-3 in the away win against Manchester City.

United finished the season in eighth place and while they reached the Semi-final of the League Cup they were eliminated from the FA Cup at their first hurdle. While Best again finished as the Club's top scorer with 18 league goals and 21 one in all competitions, disciplinary problems again tainted his season.

LEAGUE DIVISION 1			Shirt	Goals	Score
1. 15th August 1970	Leeds United	H	11		0-1
2. 19th August 1970	Chelsea	H	11		0-0
3. 22nd August 1970	Arsenal	A	11		0-4
4. 25th August 1970	Burnley	A	11		2-0
5. 29th August 1970	West Ham United	H	11		1-1
6. 2nd September 1970	Everton	H	11	1	2-0
7. 5th September 1970	Liverpool	A	11		1-1
8. 12th September 1970	Coventry City	H	11	1	2-0
9. 19th September 1970	Ipswich Town	A	11		0-4
10. 26th September 1970	Blackpool	H	11	1	1-1
11. 3rd October 1970	Wolverhampton Wanderers	A	11		2-3
12. 10th October 1970	Crystal Palace	H	8		0-1
13. 17th October 1970	Leeds United	A	8		2-2
14. 24th October 1970	West Bromwich Albion	H	8		2-1
15. 31st October 1970	Newcastle United	A	8		0-1
16. 7th November 1970	Stoke City	H	8		2-2
17. 14th November 1970	Nottingham Forest	A	8		2-1
18. 21st November 1970	Southampton	A	8		0-1
19. 28th November 1970	Huddersfield Town	H	8	1	1-1
20. 5th December 1970	Tottenham Hotspur	A	8	1	2-2
21. 12th December 1970	Manchester City	H	8		1-4
22. 19th December 1970	Arsenal	H	8		1-3
23. 26th December 1970	Derby County	A	8	1	4-4
24. 30th January 1971	Huddersfield Town	A	11		2-1
25. 6th February 1971	Tottenham Hotspur	H	11	1	2-1
26. 20th February 1971	Southampton	H	8		5-1
27. 23rd February 1971	Everton	A	8		0-1
28. 27th February 1971	Newcastle United	H	8		1-0
29. 6th March 1971	West Bromwich Albion	A	8	1	3-4
30. 13th March 1971	Nottingham Forest	H	8	1	2-0
31. 20th March 1971	Stoke City	A	8	2	2-1
32. 3rd April 1971	West Ham United	A	8	1	1-2
33. 10th April 1971	Derby County	H	8		1-2
34. 12th April 1971	Wolverhampton Wanderers	H	7		1-0
35. 13th April 1971	Coventry City	A	7	1	1-2
36. 17th April 1971	Crystal Palace	A	7	2	5-3
37. 19th April 1971	Liverpool	H	7		0-2
38. 24th April 1971	Ipswich Town	H	11	1	3-2
39. 1st May 1971	Blackpool	A	11		1-1
40. 5th May 1971	Manchester City	A	11	2	4-3

FA CUP

			Shirt	Goals	Score
1. 2nd January 1971 Round 3	Middlesbrough	H	8		0-0
2. 5th January 1971 Round 3 Replay	Middlesbrough	A	8	1	1-2

LEAGUE CUP

			Shirt	Goals	Score
1. 9th September 1970 Round 2	Aldershot	A	11	1	3-1
2. 7th October 1970 Round 3	Portsmouth	H	11		1-0
3. 28th October 1970 Round 4	Chelsea	H	8	1	2-1
4. 18th November 1970 Round 5	Crystal Palace	H	8		4-2
5. 16th December 1970 Semi-final 1st leg	Aston Villa	H	8		1-1
6. 23rd December 1970 Semi-final 2nd leg	Aston Villa	A	8		1-2

Goal versus Everton, 2nd September 1970.

Goal versus Aldershot (League Cup, Round 2), 9th September 1970.

Opposite. Goal versus Tottenham Hotspur, 6th February 1971.

Opposite. Two goals versus Stoke City, 20th March 1971.

WATNEY CUP

			Shirt	Goals	Score
1. 1st August 1970 Round 1	Reading	A	11		3-2
2. 5th August 1970 Semi-final	Hull City	A	11		1-1
3. 8th August 1970 Final	Derby County	A	11	1	1-4

FRIENDLIES

			Shirt	Goals	Score
1. 22nd March 1971	Blackburn Rovers	A	11	1	2-0
2. 25th May 1971 Austria Tour match	Klagenfurt	A	11	1	3-0
3. 28th May 1971 Austria Tour match	Styrian Provin	A	10		3-0
4. 1st June 1971 Switzerland Tour match	Zurich Grasshoppers	A	11	1	3-2

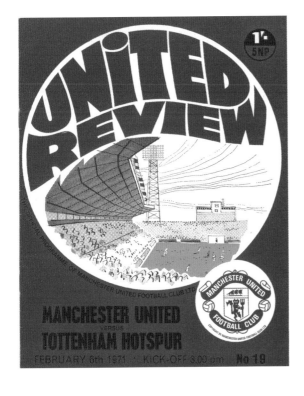

United began their new campaign brightly by winning three out of their first five league games and drawing the other two. Best chipped in with three goals during this period and then added a fourth in a 1-0 home win against Ipswich Town on the 4th September. He added two more to his tally when three days later United again played Ipswich Town in the League Cup 2nd round at Portman Road and won 3-1. George was in scintillating form when he a grabbed a hat-trick against West Ham United at home on 18th September in a 4-2 win. He followed this up with consecutive goals against Sheffield United, Huddersfield Town, Derby County and Newcastle United which all resulted in United victories and left them four points clear at the top of the table.

George recorded another treble against Southampton at The Dell in a 5-2 win on 27th November as United won four successive league games. He also scored against Stoke City in the League Cup 4th round second replay during this period though United lost 2-1. League form dipped a little before the end of the year with three consecutive draws. Results worsened at the start of 1972 when the side lost seven league games in succession with Best failing to score in any of them. Additionally, George was dropped for the home game against Wolverhampton Wanderers on 8th January after missing training. He headed to London, yet upon his return and was fined two weeks wages and instructed to do extra training. He responded by returning to first team action and scored two goals in the FA Cup 3rd round replay against Southampton at home on 19th January. He scored a further goal in the competition when United won 3-0 in the 5th round replay at Middlesbrough. Best netted again in a 2-0 home league win against Huddersfield Town on 11th March. The victory was their first in 11 matches though the side slipped to sixth place in the league.

George scored goals in each of the two FA Cup 6th round ties against Stoke City in March though United lost 2-1 at the Victoria Ground. After Best scored again against Coventry City in a 3-2 home win on 1st April United failed to win their next four league games before Best found the net in the 3-2 home win against Southampton on 15th April. The season concluded with a 3-0 home victory against Stoke City in which Best scored his 18th league goal of the season. For the fifth consecutive season George finished top goal scorer netting 26 goals in all competitions. Manchester United finished the league season in eighth place, ten points behind champions Derby County.

LEAGUE DIVISION 1

			Shirt	Goals	Score
1. 14th August 1971	Derby County	A	11		2-2
2. 18th August 1971	Chelsea	A	11		3-2
3. 20th August 1971	Arsenal	N	11		3-1
4. 23rd August 1971	West Bromwich Albion	N	10	2	3-1
5. 28th August 1971	Wolverhampton Wanderers	A	11	1	1-1
6. 31st August 1971	Everton	A	11		0-1
7. 4th September 1971	Ipswich Town	H	11	1	1-0
8. 11th September 1971	Crystal Palace	A	11		3-1
9. 18th September 1971	West Ham United	H	11	3	4-2
10. 25th September 1971	Liverpool	A	11		2-2
11. 2nd October 1971	Sheffield United	H	10	1	2 0
12. 9th October 1971	Huddersfield Town	A	11	1	3-0
13. 16th October 1971	Derby County	H	11	1	1-0
14. 23rd October 1971	Newcastle United	A	11	1	1-0
15. 30th October 1971	Leeds United	H	11		0-1
16. 6th November 1971	Manchester City	A	11		3-3
17. 13th November 1971	Tottenham Hotspur	H	11		3-1
18. 20th November 1971	Leicester City	H	11		3-2
19. 27th November 1971	Southampton	A	11	3	5-2
20. 4th December 1971	Nottingham Forest	H	11		3-2
21. 11th December 1971	Stoke City	A	11		1-1
22. 18th December 1971	Ipswich Town	A	11		0-0
23. 27th December 1971	Coventry City	H	11		2-2
24. 1st January 1972	West Ham United	A	11		0-3
25. 22nd January 1972	Chelsea	H	11		0-1
26. 29th January 1972	West Bromwich Albion	A	11		1-2
27. 12th February 1972	Newcastle United	H	11		0-2
28. 19th February 1972	Leeds United	A	11		1-5
29. 4th March 1972	Tottenham Hotspur	A	11		0-2
30. 8th March 1972	Everton	H	11		0-0
31. 11th March 1972	Huddersfield Town	H	10	1	2-0
32. 25th March 1972	Crystal Palace	H	7		4-0
33. 1st April 1972	Coventry City	A	8	1	3-2
34. 3rd April 1972	Liverpool	H	8		0-3
35. 4th April 1972	Sheffield United	A	7		1-1
36. 8th April 1972	Leicester City	A	7		0-2
37. 12th April 1972	Manchester City	H	7		1-3
38. 15th April 1972	Southampton	H	7	1	3-2
39. 25th April 1972	Arsenal	A	7		0-3
40. 29th April 1972	Stoke City	H	7	1	3-0

FA CUP

			Shirt	Goals	Score
1. 15th January 1972 Round 3	Southampton	A	11		1-1
2. 19th January 1972 Round 3 Replay	Southampton	H	11	2	4-1
3. 5th February 1972 Round 4	Preston North End	A	11		2-0
4. 26th February 1972 Round 5	Middlesbrough	H	11		0-0
5. 29th February 1972 Round 5 Replay	Middlesbrough	A	11	1	3-0
6. 18th March 1972 Round 6	Stoke City	H	11	1	1-1
7. 22nd March 1972 Round 6 Replay	Stoke City	A	11	1	1-2

LEAGUE CUP

			Shirt	Goals	Score
1. 7th September 1971 Round 2	Ipswich Town	A	10	2	3-1
2. 6th October 1971 Round 3	Burnley	H	10		1-1
3. 18th October 1971 Round 3 Replay	Burnley	A	11		1-0
4. 27th October 1971 Round 4	Stoke City	H	11		1-1
5. 8th November 1971 Round 4 Replay	Stoke City	A	11		0-0
6. 15th November 1971 Round 4 Second Replay	Stoke City	A	11	1	1-2

*Hat-trick versus West Ham United,
18th September 1971.*

*Goal versus Newcastle United, 23rd
October 1971.*

*Opposite. Hat-trick versus
Southampton, 27th November 1971.*

*Opposite. Two goals versus
Southampton (FA Cup, Round 3
Replay), 19th January 1971.*

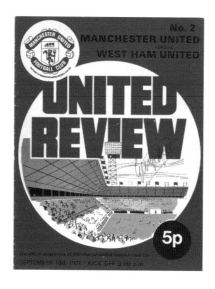

WATNEY CUP

			Shirt	Goals	Score
1. 31st July 1971 Round 1	Halifax Town	A	11	1	1-2

FRIENDLIES

			Shirt	Goals	Score
1. 4th August 1971	Luton Town	A	11		2-0
2. 7th August 1971	Fulham	A	11	1	1-2
3. 9th August 1971	Coventry City	H	11	1	3-1
4. 30th November 1971	St Ouens	A	11	1	4-0
5. 3rd May 1972 Alan Oakes Testimonial	Manchester City	A	10		3-1

Perhaps the poor end to the previous season should have alerted those within the club that all was far from well on the playing field. The 1971 / 72 season had ended with the team winning just three of their last eight league games. The older members of the team were on a slow decline and were no longer the influential figures that they once were.

The new season started badly with the team losing their first three games and failing to win any of their first nine league matches. Best scored goals in drawn games at home to Leicester City and away to West Ham United before netting two more at home to Oxford United in the League Cup 2nd round replay though United were knocked out of the competition 2-1 by Third Division Bristol Rovers in the 3rd round replay at Old Trafford

Best scored again in a 2-2 away draw at West Bromwich Albion on 7th October though the result left United bottom of the table. The remainder of October included a 2-1 away defeat at Newcastle United and a 4-1 home loss against Tottenham Hotspur. George scored in a 2-2 draw at Leicester City on 4th November though this proved to be his final goal of the season. Following a humiliating 3-0 defeat at Manchester City on 18th November United returned to the bottom of the league. Best played in the next league game the following week at home to Southampton which United won 2-1. He missed training early the next week and Frank O'Farrell suspended him for two weeks. Best again headed to London while United won their next match 2-0 at home to Norwich City on 2nd December. Sadly, the team lost the next match 2-0 at home to Stoke City and were then humiliated 5-0 at Crystal Palace on 16th December. Frank O'Farrell was sacked as a result and on the day of his dismissal a letter was received by the United directors from Best saying that he was finished with football.

George went away to contemplate a life away from football while Manchester United appointed Tommy Docherty as their new manager. Results slowly improved under Docherty's leadership and United narrowly managed to avoid relegation. Best meanwhile, spent his summer relaxing in Marbella where he pondered his future.

Goal versus Leicester City, 23rd August 1972.

Goal versus West Ham United, 2nd September 1972.

Two goals versus Oxford United (League Cup, Round 2, Replay), 12th September 1972.

Goal versus West Bromwich Albion, 7th October 1972.

LEAGUE DIVISION 1

			Shirt	Goals	Score
1. 12th August 1972	Ipswich Town	H	7		1-2
2. 15th August 1972	Liverpool	A	10		0-2
3. 19th August 1972	Everton	A	10		0-2
4. 23rd August 1972	Leicester City	H	10	1	1-1
5. 26th August 1972	Arsenal	H	10		0-0
6. 30th August 1972	Chelsea	H	10		0-0
7. 2nd September 1972	West Ham United	A	10	1	2-2
8. 9th September 1972	Coventry City	H	10		0-1
9. 16th September 1972	Wolverhampton Wanderers	A	10		0-2
10. 23rd September 1972	Derby County	H	10		3-0
11. 30th September 1972	Sheffield United	A	10		0-1
12. 7th October 1972	West Bromwich Albion	A	10	1	2-2
13. 14th October 1972	Birmingham City	H	10		1-0
14. 21st October 1972	Newcastle United	A	10		1-2
15. 28th October 1972	Tottenham Hotspur	H	10		1-4
16. 4th November 1972	Leicester City	A	7	1	2-2
17. 11th November 1972	Liverpool	H	7		2-0
18. 18th November 1972	Manchester City	A	7		0-3
19. 25th November 1972	Southampton	H	7		2-1

LEAGUE CUP

			Shirt	Goals	Score
1. 6th September 1972 Round 2	Oxford United	A	10		2-2
2. 12th September 1972 Round 2 Replay	Oxford United	H	10	2	3-1
3. 3rd October 1972 Round 3	Bristol Rovers	A	10		1-1
4. 11th October 1972 Round 3 Replay	Bristol Rovers	H	10		1-2

FRIENDLIES

			Shirt	Goals	Score
1. 23rd October 1972	Aberdeen	A	11		2-5
2. 13th November 1972 Ron Boyce Testimonial	West Ham United	A	7		2-5

During the summer of 1973 George Best declared that he would not play football again. However, in late August United Chairman Louis Edwards stated that he would like the Irishman to begin training with the Club. Tommy Docherty was also keen to have Best back in a side which had avoided relegation by seven points the previous season. Following talks between the two, Best announced that he would like to give football another try. When he reported for training on 10th September United had lost three of their opening five league games and another season of struggle beckoned.

After 10 months out of the game Best was unfit and desperately short of match practise. He began training and played in a series of less demanding games in a bid to get fit. Best played for 45 minutes for Benfica in Eusebio's testimonial match in Lisbon on 25th September and then played for United in Denis Law's testimonial game eight days later. On 6th October George turned out for United's reserve team for the first time in almost ten years. A crowd of 7,126 saw United lose 2-0 to Aston Villa reserves. On 15th October Best played for United in an away friendly at Shamrock Rovers. George made his return to competitive action on 20th October in a 1-0 home win against Birmingham City. Unfortunately the team didn't manage to win any of their next nine league games though Best scored goals in the 2-1 defeat at Tottenham Hotspur and the 3-2 loss against Coventry City at Old Trafford. Sadly George's acceleration had gone and he was now a shadow of his former self playing in a poor team.

United defeated Ipswich Town 2-0 at home on 29th December and yet it proved to be George's final competitive match at Old Trafford. On New Years Day the team played at Queens Park Rangers and were beaten 3-0. It was a result which left United in the relegation zone. More significantly it was Best's last game in a United shirt. Two days later he failed to turn up for training and his time at Old Trafford was all but finished. George arrived to play in United's FA Cup third round tie against Plymouth Argyle on 5th January. Following an altercation with Tommy Docherty Best was dropped from the team. He walked away from Old Trafford for the final time and turned his back on a twelve and a half year career at United. Sadly, the writing for Best had been on the wall for a long time. Meanwhile, the side he left behind suffered inevitable relegation.

First reserve appearance for 10 years versus Aston Villa, 6th October 1973.

First team comeback game versus Birmingham City, 20th October 1973.

Last home appearance for Manchester United versus Ipswich Town, 29th December 1973.

Last appearance for Manchester United versus Queens Park Rangers, 1st January 1974.

RESERVES – CENTRAL LEAGUE

			Shirt	Goals	Score
1. 6th October 1973	Aston Villa	H	7		0-2

LEAGUE DIVISION 1

			Shirt	Goals	Score
1. 20th October 1973	Birmingham City	H	11		1-0
2. 27th October 1973	Burnley	A	11		0-0
3. 3rd November 1973	Chelsea	H	11		2-2
4. 10th November 1973	Tottenham Hotspur	A	11	1	1-2
5. 17th November 1973	Newcastle United	A	11		2-3
6. 24th November 1973	Norwich City	H	11		0-0
7. 8th December 1973	Southampton	H	11		0-0
8. 15th December 1973	Coventry City	H	11	1	2-3
9. 22nd December 1973	Liverpool	A	11		0-2
10. 26th December 1973	Sheffield United	H	11		1-2
11. 29th December 1973	Ipswich Town	H	11		2-0
12. 1st January 1974	Queens Park Rangers	A	11		0-3

FRIENDLIES

			Shirt	Goals	Score
1. 3rd October 1973 Denis Law Testimonial	Ajax	H	11		1-0
2. 15th October 1973	Shamrock Rovers	A	11		2-1
3. 24th October 1973 Tony Dunne Testimonial	Manchester City	H	11	1	1-2
4. 5th November 1973 Donnie McKinnon Testimonial	Partick Thistle	A	11		3-0
5. 4th December 1973	Portsmouth	A	11		1-1
6. 12th December 1973 Gordon Banks Testimonial	Stoke City	A	11		2-1

The month following Manchester United's relegation to the Second Division George Best signed a lucrative short term deal to play for Johannesburg based Jewish Guild. While Best had not played competitive football for five months his arrival in South Africa generated considerable interest.

The BP League officials assisted Jewish Guild by rearranging fixtures to help maximise the ailing club's takings and to ensure that Best was seen by as many football fans as possible. However, the Irishman struggled with his fitness and the deal did not prove to be the huge success which was envisaged. Jewish Guild managed to win just one of the four games in which Best played. He figured in a 2-0 away victory to Durban City on 2nd June having played two days earlier in a home game against Hellenic which ended in a 1-1 draw. On the 5th June Best played in the return fixture in Hellenic though Guild were beaten 5-1. George's fourth and final appearance came in a home game against Durban United 48 hours later. Best scored Guild's only goal though his team lost the game 2-1. It was a whirlwind seven days of football for George and while he benefitted financially his displays proved a disappointment.

Penultimate appearance for Jewish Guild versus Hellenic, 5th June 1974.

Souvenir programme (front and back) issued to commemorate appearances for Jewish Guild.

Opposite. Debut for Dunstable Town versus Manchester United, 5th August 1974.

Opposite. Second game for Dunstable Town versus Cork Celtic, 12th August 1974.

Opposite. Jeff Astle Testimonial. Appearance for WBA '68 versus WBA '74, 29th October 1974.

Opposite. Tony Book Testimonial. Appearance for All Stars XI versus Manchester City XI, 27th November 1974.

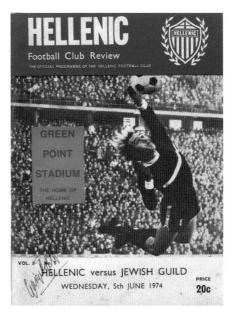

THE R15 000 BP LEAGUE			Shirt	Goals	Score
1. 31st May 1974	Hellenic	H	11		1-1
2. 2nd June 1974	Durban City	A	11		2-0
3. 5th June 1974	Hellenic	A	11		1-5
4. 7th June 1974	Durban United	H	11	1	1-2

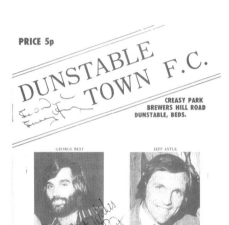

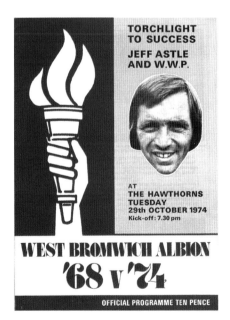

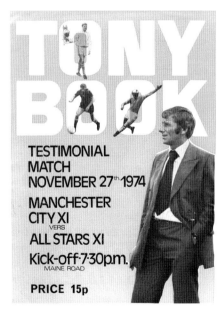

George Best's long association with Manchester United finally came to an end when he was released from his Old Trafford contract on 8th November 1975. Since leaving United early in 1974 Best had appeared for Jewish Guild, played three games for Dunstable Town and turned out in a handful of testimonial games. On 10th November 1975 George signed a short term contract to play home games for Fourth Division Stockport County. The Edgeley Park club was struggling in the re-election places but Best's signing again caused considerable media interest. His first appearance came on the day of his signing when he appeared in a home friendly against Stoke City. The match attracted a crowd of 8,081 which was an increase of 5,000 spectators on their previous home game. To the delight of those who attended, a slightly heavier Best turned on the style and hit the bar twice during the match. The highlight came when he scored a fine second half goal from a free kick as the match ended in a 1-1 draw.

Best's reappearance in league football alerted bigger clubs and Stoke City, Queens Park Rangers and Southampton were all reported as being interested in signing the player. On 24th November George guested for Chelsea in Peter Osgood's testimonial and scored twice. Speculation followed that Best would join the west London side though subsequent reports declared that Chelsea were reluctant to meet his wage demands. Best made an emotional return to Old Trafford two days later to play in Pat Crerand's testimonial match.

Best returned to Stockport and made his full league debut for County on 28th November in front of 9,220 spectators. Representatives of seven First Division clubs witnessed George play a part in all three of County's goals in their 3-2 win against Swansea City. A dangerous in swinging Best corner resulted in goalkeeper Steve Potter fumbling the ball into his own net. A fine pass from George allowed Lee Bradley to fire home and then Best scored himself with a left foot shot just inside the penalty box. Rumours surfaced once more that Chelsea were interested in signing the Irishman on a match fee basis which was linked to attendances. Best though played in his second league game against Watford and scored again in a 2-2 draw. His Stockport career ended after his third and final league appearance against Southport on Boxing Day morning. It was a game which County won 1-0. Best left Edgeley Park and signed a contract play for Los Angeles Aztecs in the 1976 North American Soccer League Season.

FRIENDLY			Shirt	Goals	Score
1. 10th November 1975	Stoke City	H	11	1	1-1

LEAGUE DIVISION 4			Shirt	Goals	Score
1. 28th November 1975	Swansea City	H	7	1	3-2
2. 12th December 1975	Watford	H	11	1	2-2
3. 26th December 1975	Southport	H	11		1-0

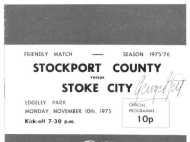

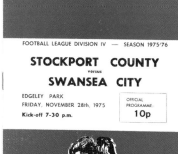

Friendly debut for Stockport County versus Stoke City, 10th November 1975.

League debut for Stockport County versus Swansea City, 28th November 1975.

Third game for Stockport County versus Watford, 12th December 1975.

Final game for Stockport County versus Southport, 26th December 1975.

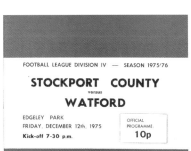

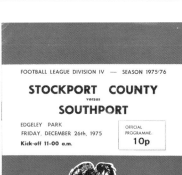

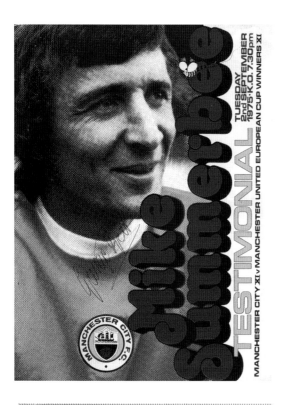

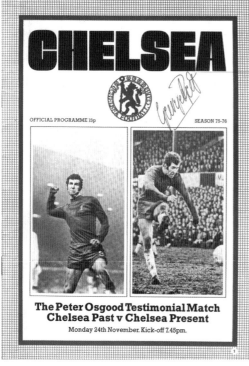

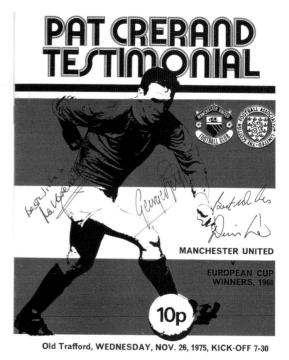

It came as a surprise to many when George Best flew from Manchester to Dublin on 27th December 1975 to sign for Cork Celtic. Manager Paul O'Donovan probably could not have believed his luck in acquiring the services of 29 year old Best. He linked up with Bobby Tambling formerly of Chelsea, Crystal Palace and England.

Best's first game was played the day after he signed for Cork. The interest in the game caused the match to be switched from Cork's Turner's Cross ground to the larger Flower Lodge venue. A crowd of 12,000 witnessed George and his team mates lose 2-0 to Drogheda. His next appearance was back at Cork's usual home ground before a crowd of 9,000. Best put in an average performance as his side triumphed 1-0 against Bohemians. The following week Best and Cork travelled to Dublin to play Shelbourne. A record crowd of 7,000 attended to see the home team win 2-1. Many thought that George's performances were lacklustre and not worthy of the reported £600 a game which he was receiving. The following day Best was sacked by his club for 'his lack of enthusiasm'.

Opposite. Mike Summerbee Testimonial. Appearance for Manchester United European Cup Winners XI versus Manchester City XI, 2nd September 1975.

Opposite. Final appearance for Dunstable Town versus Luton Town, 29th October 1975.

Opposite. Peter Osgood Testimonial. Appearance for Chelsea Past versus Chelsea Present, 24th November 1975.

Opposite. Pat Crerand Testimonial. Appearance for European Cup Winners 1968 versus Manchester United, 26th November 1975.

BASS LEAGUE OF IRELAND				Shirt	Goals	Score
1. 28th December 1975	Drogheda United	H		10		0-2
2. 11th January 1976	Bohemians	H		9		1-0
3. 18th January 1976	Shelbourne	A		7		1-2

New York Cosmos had shown interest in signing George Best in December 1972 and they approached Manchester United the following month for permission to talk to him. Planned negotiations though came to nothing and it was not until three years later that George decided to play in the North American Soccer League when he signed for Los Angeles Aztecs in December 1975.

Best began training with his new team mates on 20th February 1976 and made his debut for the Aztecs on 17th April. A crowd of 19,807 attended the Spartan Stadium to witness George's new side lose 2-1 at San Jose Earthquakes. The following week fortunes improved both for Best and his Los Angeles team. George scored the only goal in a home win against Rochester Lancers. Sadly, the game was attended by a poor crowd of only 7,236 spectators to witness George's home debut. Best scored again in the next Aztecs game in a 2-0 home win against San Diego Jaws on 2nd May. He then scored a further goal in an exciting 4-3 home win against Seattle Sounders. On 17th May the Aztecs visited the Yankee Stadium in New York and were heavily beaten 6-0 by a Pele inspired Cosmos.

Best scored the only goal of the game on 5th June in a home win against Portland Timbers and then netted in a 2-1 win in the next match at home to Vancouver Whitecaps. He scored two goals in each of the Aztecs' next two games against Tampa Bay Rowdies which his side won 2-1 and the 6-3 defeat at Dallas Tornado on 20th June. George failed to score in the next three games until finding the net once in a 2-1 home win against St Louis Stars on 10th July and again six days later at San Diego Jaws by the same scoreline. On 18th July Los Angeles Aztecs achieved their biggest win of the season when they thrashed Boston Minutemen 8-0 at home with Best scoring his first and only Hat-trick in the NASL. Unfortunately, the fine win was followed by four consecutive defeats including a 6-2 hammering at Minnesota Kicks on 10th August. Best scored in the final game of the season four days later in a 4-1 home win against Dallas Tornado. The Aztecs reached the Play-offs where they again played the Dallas franchise but lost the match 2-0 away.

George Best's first season in the NASL had proved a success. He missed just one of the Aztecs 25 games and scored 15 goals with seven assists making him the side's top goals and points scorer. On a disappointing note Los Angeles Aztecs average home attendance totalled 8,027.

NASL PACIFIC CONFERENCE SOUTHERN DIVISION

			Shirt	Goals	Score
1. 17th April 1976	San Jose Earthquakes	A	11		1-2
2. 25th April 1976	Rochester Lancers	H	11	1	1-0
3. 2nd May 1976	San Diego Jaws	H	11	1	2-0
4. 8th May 1976	San Antonio Thunder	A	11		2-3
5. 9th May 1976	Seattle Sounders	H	11	1	4-3
6. 14th May 1976	Philadelphia Atoms	A	11		2-1
7. 17th May 1976	New York Cosmos	A	11		0-6
8. 2nd June 1976	Toronto Metros-Croatia	A	11		0-2
9. 5th June 1976	Portland Timbers	H	11	1	1-0
10. 12th June 1976	Vancouver Whitecaps	H	11	1	2-1
11. 19th June 1976	Tampa Bay Rowdies	H	11	2	2-1
12. 20th June 1976	Dallas Tornado	A	11	2	3-6
13. 26th June 1976	Minnesota Kicks	H	11		0-1
14. 3rd July 1976	San Antonio Thunder	A	11		1-2
15. 5th July 1976	Portland Timbers	A	11		2-1
16. 10th July 1976	St Louis Stars	H	11	1	2-1
17. 16th July 1976	San Diego Jaws	A	11	1	2-1
18. 18th July 1976	Boston Minutemen	H	11	3	8-0
19. 23rd July 1976	Vancouver Whitecaps	A	11		1-2
20. 25th July 1976	San Jose Earthquakes	H	11		0-1
21. 31st July 1976	Seattle Sounders	A	11		0-1
22. 10th August 1976	Minnesota Kicks	A	11		2-6
23. 14th August 1976	Dallas Tornado	H	11	1	4-1

PLAY-OFF

			Shirt	Goals	Score
1. 18th August 1976	Dallas Tornado	A	11		0-2

On 12th August 1976 George Best signed a contract to play for Second Division Fulham. He made his return to English football on 4th September in the home game against Bristol Rovers. A crowd of 21,127 gathered to watch not only Best's league debut but that of Rodney Marsh formerly of Queens Park Rangers and Manchester City. The partnership got off to a superb start when Best fired Fulham into a 71 second lead which proved to be the only goal of the game.

Best and Fulham travelled to Peterborough United three days later and he scored again with a thirty yard volley in the League Cup 2nd round replay. Fulham won the match 2-1 and progressed to the 3rd round. The Cottagers remained unbeaten during September and after a 4-1 win against Hereford United on 25th September they moved up to fourth place in the league. Three days earlier George had scored again in a home League Cup 3rd round tie against Bolton Wanderers which ended in a 2-2 draw. Unfortunately, on 2nd October Best was sent off at Southampton for using foul and abusive language. His team crashed 4-1 and George was later fined £75 by an FA disciplinary commission. The rest of October proved to be a poor month as Fulham failed to win though Best did score in a 2-1 defeat at Bolton Wanderers on 30th October. He netted a further goal against Cardiff City in a 2-1 home defeat but it proved to George's only goal during November as Fulham slipped to 15th place.

On 4th December Fulham thrashed Oldham Athletic 5-0 as Best scored again and he also found the target against Blackburn Rovers on 14th December in a 2-0 home win. Fulham lost their next four league games though Best missed two of them due to badly bruised legs which he sustained in a 2-0 defeat at Chelsea on 27th December. George was back in action for a 2-0 home defeat against Bolton Wanderers on the 3rd January and then he appeared against Swindon Town at Craven Cottage in the FA Cup 3rd round. The match was drawn 3-3 though Fulham lost the replay 5-0 three days later. The Cottagers failed to win any of their next eight league games. The sequence included a 3-0 defeat at Nottingham Forest on 22nd January and a 5-1 defeat at Wolverhampton Wanderers on 19th February. Five days after the loss at Molineux Best was involved in a car accident in Knightsbridge which hospitalised him and forced him to miss the next five games.

George returned to first team action on 2nd April and appeared in a 1-0 defeat at Hull City. He was also given a run out in the reserve team two days later at home to Hereford United. Fulham's form had caused them to slip to 18th position in the league. Fortunes improved when Best scored in the next game against Chelsea at Craven Cottage on 8th April. The 3-1 win sparked an improvement in results as Fulham lost just two of their last seven league games. The team finished 17th in the league and avoided relegation by two points. The signings of Best and Marsh had brought considerable interest to Craven Cottage though the results had proved extremely erratic. Best had contributed eight goals in 37 games.

LEAGUE DIVISION 2

			Shirt	Goals	Score
1. 4th September 1976	Bristol Rovers	H	7	1	1-0
2. 11th September 1976	Wolverhampton Wanderers	H	7		0-0
3. 18th September 1976	Luton Town	A	7		2-0
4. 25th September 1976	Hereford United	H	7		4-1
5. 2nd October 1976	Southampton	A	7		1-4
6. 16th October 1976	Sheffield United	A	7		1-1
7. 23rd October 1976	Hull City	H	7		0-0
8. 30th October 1976	Bolton Wanderers	A	7	1	1-2
9. 6th November 1976	Cardiff City	H	7	1	1-2
10. 13th November 1976	Plymouth Argyle	A	7		2-2
11. 16th November 1976	Carlisle United	H	7		2-0
12. 20th November 1976	Notts County	H	7		1-5
13. 27th November 1976	Blackpool	A	7		2-3
14. 4th December 1976	Oldham Athletic	H	7	1	5-0
15. 11th December 1976	Orient	A	7		0-0
16. 14th December 1976	Blackburn Rovers	H	7	1	2-0
17. 27th December 1976	Chelsea	A	7		0-2
18. 3rd January 1977	Bolton Wanderers	H	7		0-2
19. 15th January 1977	Burnley	H	7		2-2
20. 22nd January 1977	Nottingham Forest	A	7		0-3
21. 5th February 1977	Charlton Athletic	H	7		1-1
22. 12th February 1977	Bristol Rovers	A	7		1-2
23. 19th February 1977	Wolverhampton Wanderers	A	7		1-5
24. 2nd April 1977	Hull City	A	7		0-1
25. 8th April 1977	Chelsea	H	7	1	3-1
26. 9th April 1977	Millwall	A	7		0-0
27. 11th April 1977	Plymouth Argyle	H	7		2-0
28. 16th April 1977	Notts County	A	7		0-0
29. 23rd April 1977	Blackpool	H	7		0-0
30. 30th April 1977	Oldham Athletic	A	7		0-1
31. 7th May 1977	Orient	H	7		6-1
32. 14th May 1977	Blackburn Rovers	A	7		0-1

RESERVES – FOOTBALL COMBINATION

			Shirt	Goals	Score
1. 4th April 1977	Hereford United	H	10		1-3

FA CUP

			Shirt	Goals	Score
1. 8th January 1977 Round 3	Swindon Town	H	7		3-3
2. 11th January 1977 Round 3 Replay	Swindon Town	A	7		0-5

LEAGUE CUP

			Shirt	Goals	Score
1. 7th September 1976 Round 2 Replay	Peterborough United	A	7	1	2-1
2. 22nd September 1976 Round 3	Bolton Wanderers	H	7	1	2-2
3. 18th October 1976 Round 3 Second Replay	Bolton Wanderers	N	7		1-2

FRIENDLIES

			Shirt	Goals	Score
1. 26th October 1976	Redhill	A	7	1	6-2
2. 2nd November 1976 Frank Lampard Testimonial	West Ham United	A	7		1-3
3. 23rd November 1976 Les Barrett Testimonial	West Ham United	H	7		2-5
4. 30th January 1977	Guernsey Select XI	A	7		3-1

SIX-A-SIDE TOURNAMENT IN BRONDBY HALLEN, COPENHAGEN, DENMARK

		Shirt	Goals	Score
1. 28th March 1977 Round 1	Sweden	n/k	1	2-9
2. 27th March 1977 3rd and 4th Place play off	Denmark	n/k	5	9-11

SIX-A-SIDE TOURNAMENT IN RANDERS HALLEN, RANDERS, JUTLAND

		Shirt	Goals	Score
1. 29th March 1977 Round 1	Sweden	n/k	2	5-2
2. 29th March 1977 Final	Fulham	n/k	2	8-2

Fulham entered two squads for the above tournament. Best appeared in the squad called Fulham Best & Co.

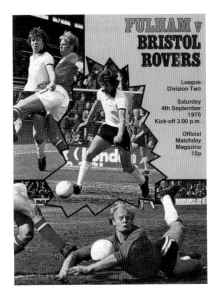

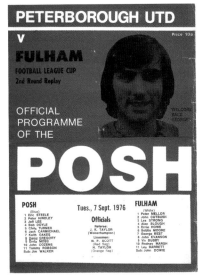

League debut for Fulham versus Bristol Rovers, 4th September 1976.

Goal versus Peterborough United (League Cup Round 2 Replay) 7th September 1976.

Sent off in away league game at Southampton, 8th October 1976.

Goal versus Redhill (friendly) 26th October 1976.

Goal versus Chelsea, 2nd April 1977.

Final appearance of the season versus Blackburn Rovers, 14th May 1977.

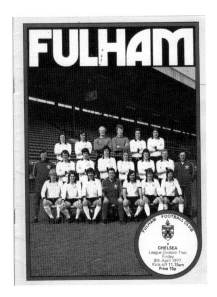

George Best's second season with the Aztecs overlapped with the end of the English season and he missed the first the first six games of the new NASL season. He played his first game of the new campaign in a 1-0 defeat at Portland Timbers on 20th May. Following the result the Aztecs won their next six games in succession with Best scoring goals in successive games against Seattle Sounders, St Louis Stars, Dallas Tornado, Las Vegas Quicksilver and Minnesota Kicks. Unfortunately, the fine run ended with a 4-3 defeat at Rochester Lancers on 22nd June. A further loss followed in the next game at New York Cosmos. Defeat also followed in the next game at New York Cosmos. Pele scored a Hat-trick in the 5-2 win with Best scoring one of the Aztecs goals in front of a 57,191 crowd.

Best's team won three out of their next seven matches with George scoring just one goal during the sequence. On 22nd July he netted against Team Hawaii in an away match which the Aztecs lost 6-5. It was unfortunate that only 6,392 spectators witnessed the spectacle. Best scored again in the next fixture away at Las Vegas Quicksilver which saw his side triumph 3-2. George followed this by scoring in successive games at home to San Jose Earthquakes, away to Vancouver Whitecaps and finally at home to Seattle Sounders. Fifteen wins from 26 games proved enough for the Aztecs to reach the Play-offs.

The first game saw Best score in a 2-1 home win against San Jose Earthquakes on 10th August though the game was watched by a paltry crowd of just 4,038. Home and away victories followed against Dallas Tornado with George finding the back of the net in the away game as the Aztecs triumphed 5-1. Sadly the momentum could not be maintained and successive defeats followed against Seattle Sounders which ended the Aztecs season.

Best had played in 25 successive games of the campaign and contributed 11 goals with 18 assists in the regular season and two goals with eight assists in the play-offs. His total of 40 points was only behind that of team mate Steve David with 58 points and Derek Smethurst of Tampa Bay Rowdies who secured two more points than George. Meanwhile the Los Angeles home attendances had improved slightly to an average of 8,988.

Los Angeles Aztecs Media Guide 1977.

Los Angeles Aztecs versus Dallas Tornado, Play-off, 14th August 1977.

NASL PACIFIC CONFERENCE SOUTHERN DIVISION

			Shirt	Goals	Score
1. 20th May 1977	Portland Timbers	A	11		0-1
2. 22nd May 1977	Vancouver Whitecaps	H	11		3-1
3. 28th May 1977	Seattle Sounders	A	11	1	2-1
4. 30th May 1977	St Louis Stars	H	11	1	3-2
5. 5th June 1977	Dallas Tornado	H	11	1	4-3
6. 12th June 1977	Las Vegas Quicksilver	H	11	1	3-0
7. 19th June 1977	Minnesota Kicks	A	11	1	3-2
8. 22nd June 1977	Rochester Lancers	A	11		3-4
9. 26th June 1977	New York Cosmos	A	11	1	2-5
10. 29th June 1977	Connecticut Bi-Centenn	A	11		3-2
11. 2nd July 1977	New York Cosmos	H	11		4-1
12. 4th July 1977	Toronto Metros-Croatia	H	11		0-2
13. 9th July 1977	Washington Diplomats	A	11		4-2
14. 13th July 1977	Tampa Bay Rowdies	A	11		1-4
15. 17th July 1977	Fort Lauderdale Strikers	H	11		1-3
16. 22nd July 1977	Team Hawaii	A	11	1	5-6
17. 27th July 1977	Las Vegas Quicksilver	A	11	1	3-2
18. 30th July 1977	San Jose Earthquakes	H	11	1	2-3
19. 4th August 1977	Vancouver Whitecaps	A	11	1	2-0
20. 7th August 1977	Seattle Sounders	H	11	1	2-4

PLAY-OFFS

			Shirt	Goals	Score
1. 10th August 1977	San Jose Earthquakes	H	11	1	2-1
2. 14th August 1977	Dallas Tornado	H	11		3-1
3. 17th August 1977	Dallas Tornado	A	11	1	5-1
4. 21st August 1977	Seattle Sounders	H	11		1-3
5. 25th August 1977	Seattle Sounders	A	11		0-1

George Best returned from America to play his first game of the 1977 / 78 season against Blackburn Rovers at home on 3rd September 1977. It was The Cottagers fourth league game of the season and yet they had managed to score only one goal in the previous three games without securing a win. It came as little surprise when the Blackburn game finished goalless. George missed the next two games against Tottenham Hotspur and Notts County before returning to the side to figure in a 3-1 defeat at Cardiff City. He played in a 3-2 away win at Crystal Palace and then scored his first goal of the season in a 4-1 home win against Burnley on 4th October. A 1-1 home draw followed against Blackpool before three successive defeats against Luton Town, Orient and Sheffield United left Fulham in 15th place.

On 5th November George said farewell to the Fulham fans as he played his penultimate game for the club and scored in a 3-3 draw against Sunderland. The following Saturday Best appeared in his final game for the Cottagers as Fulham lost 2-0 at Stoke City. The result left Fulham in 16th place. Best had appeared in just 10 league games before he left to return to Florida.

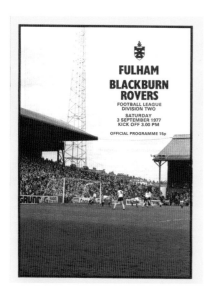
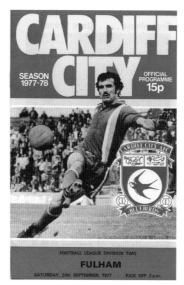
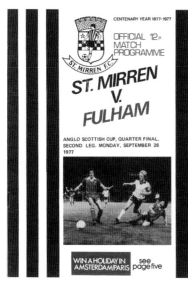

LEAGUE DIVISION 2			Shirt	Goals	Score
1. 3rd September 1977	Blackburn Rovers	H	7		0-0
2. 24th September 1977	Cardiff City	A	7		1-3
3. 1st October 1977	Crystal Palace	A	7		3-2
4. 4th October 1977	Burnley	H	7	1	4-1
5. 8th October 1977	Blackpool	H	7		1-1
6. 15th October 1977	Luton Town	A	7		0-1
7. 22nd October 1977	Orient	H	7		1-2
8. 29th October 1977	Sheffield United	A	7		1-2
9. 5th November 1977	Sunderland	H	7	1	3-3
10. 12th November 1977	Stoke City	A	7		0-2

ANGLO SCOTTISH CUP			Shirt	Goals	Score
1. 26th September 1977 Quarter-final 2nd leg	St Mirren	A	7	1	3-5

FRIENDLY			Shirt	Goals	Score
1. 6th November 1977	Guernsey Select XI	A	7		4-0

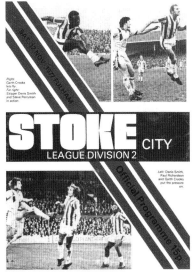

Opposite. First game of the new season versus Blackburn Rovers, 3rd September 1977.

Opposite. Appearance versus Cardiff City, 24th September 1977.

Opposite. Sole appearance in Anglo Scottish Cup versus St Mirren (Quarter-final, 2nd leg), 26th September 1977.

Opposite. Appearance versus Sheffield United, 29th October 1977.

Penultimate appearance versus Sunderland, 5th November 1977.

Final appearance for Fulham versus Stoke City, 12th November 1977.

Los Angeles Aztecs Press Guide 1978.

George Best played in the first game of the 1978 NASL season for the Aztecs in a 3-2 defeat against Houston Hurricane on 2nd April. Unfortunately, in George's first six games they failed to win only one match and lost the other five. Best missed the next two games which saw 2-1 away wins against Oakland Stompers and Chicago Sting. He returned to the side on 18th May for a 1-0 away victory at Tulsa Roughnecks. Best missed the next match at home to Dallas Tornado which saw his side lose 2-1. He returned for a 2-1 away win at Colorado Caribous. George scored his only goal of the season two days later at home to Portland Timbers on 29th May though his side lost 4-1. He played in three of the next five fixtures missing home games against Philadelphia Fury and Rochester Lancers. Best appeared in a 1-0 defeat at Portland Timbers on 7th June and in a 2-1 home win against California Surf on 17th June. His final game for the Aztecs came in a 4-0 defeat at Washington Diplomats on 20th June 1978.

Best witnessed Los Angeles Aztecs lose 10 of their first 17 games. He appeared in 12 games and scored once though he did not register a single assist. George decided to move on and join Fort Lauderdale Strikers.

NASL NATIONAL CONFERENCE WESTERN DIVISION			Shirt	Goals	Score
1. 2nd April 1978	Houston Hurricane	H	11		2-3
2. 9th April 1978	New York Cosmos	H	11		0-1
3. 16th April 1978	California Surf	A	11		4-1
4. 22nd April 1978	Fort Lauderdale Strikers	A	11		0-2
5. 30th April 1978	Oakland Stompers	H	11		1-2
6. 7th May 1978	Seattle Sounders	H	11		0-2
7. 18th May 1978	Tulsa Roughnecks	A	11		1-0
8. 27th May 1978	Colorado Caribous	A	11		2-1
9. 29th May 1978	Portland Timbers	H	11	1	1-4
10. 7th June 1978	Portland Timbers	A	11		0-1
11. 17th June 1978	California Surf	H	11		2-1
12. 20th June 1978	Washington Diplomats	A	11		0-4

George Best made his home debut at the Lockhart Stadium, Fort Lauderdale on 24th June and scored twice in a 5-3 win against New York Cosmos. The side also won their next four games against Memphis Rogues, San Jose Earthquakes, Toronto Metros-Croatia and Houston Hurricane. Defeat came in George's sixth appearance for his new side when they lost 5-0 at California Surf on 12th July.

Best missed Strikers' 4-3 defeat at home to Chicago Sting on 15th July but returned for a 2-0 win four days later at New England Tea Men. He was again absent for a 1-0 home win against Philadelphia Fury on 21st July and a 2-1 away defeat at Tampa Bay Rowdies in the next game. Best returned to score in a 4-2 loss at Detroit Express and also netted against Rochester Lancers in a 2-1 home win.

The Strikers results during the 1978 season proved sufficient to take them into the Play-offs. Victory came in the first two of these against New England Tea Men 3-1 away followed by a 4-3 home win against Detroit Express. Unfortunately, a 1-0 defeat followed in the return at Detroit. Best scored in the next game against Tampa Bay Rowdies in a 3-2 home win. A 3-1 defeat followed in the return game in Tampa and lost the tie by virtue of a shoot out. George played in all five of the Play-off games scoring one goal with two assists. In the regular season he appeared in nine games scoring four goals with one assist which had proved a useful contribution to the Strikers unsuccessful bid to win the 1978 Soccer Bowl.

NASL AMERICAN CONFERENCE EASTERN DIVISION			Shirt	Goals	Score
1. 24th June 1978	New York Cosmos	H	3	2	5-3
2. 28th June 1978	Memphis Rogues	A	3		2-1
3. 1st July 1978	San Jose Earthquakes	A	3		1-0
4. 4th July 1978	Toronto Metros-Croatia	H	3		4-0
5. 9th July 1978	Houston Hurricane	A	3		2-1
6. 12th July 1978	California Surf	A	3		0-5
7. 19th July 1978	New England Tea Men	A	3		2-0
8. 30th July 1978	Detroit Express	A	3	1	2-4
9. 4th August 1978	Rochester Lancers	H	3	1	2-1

PLAY-OFFS			Shirt	Goals	Score
1. 9th August 1978	New England Tea Men	A	3		3-1
2. 13th August 1978	Detroit Express	H	3		4-3
3. 16th August 1978	Detroit Express	A	3		0-1
4. 20th August 1978	Tampa Bay Rowdies	H	3	1	3-2
5. 23rd August 1978	Tampa Bay Rowdies	A	3		1-3

George Best began his 1979 season for Strikers in their second game of the season at home to New England Tea Men which resulted in a 2-0 win. The next game away at Toronto Blizzard saw a 2-1 win though The Strikers lost their next four games. The next win came on 12th May when Best's team beat Toronto Blizzard 4-0 at home. He appeared in only one of the next five games against Memphis Rogues on 26th May and played again against San Jose Earthquakes on 16th June. George's first goal of the season was scored against Tulsa Roughnecks on 20th June which saw a 3-2 home win for his team. A further win followed three days later when the side won 2-1 at Tampa Bay Rowdies.

On 27th June The Strikers travelled to Detroit Express where they were heavily beaten 8-2. George did not play in the next game at home to Vancouver Whitecaps three days later but the side bounced back without him and won 3-2. The Irishman returned on 4th July for a game at home to Chicago Sting but could not prevent The Strikers from losing 3-2. He figured in the next two games at San Jose Earthquakes and San Diego Sockers which both ended in victories for Best's team. Three defeats followed though George scored in the third of these at Portland Timbers though his team lost 4-1. He played his final game for Fort Lauderdale Strikers away to California Surf on 25th July and helped the team to a 6-3 win.

The Strikers reached the Play-offs but George missed the final five games of the regular season and took no part in the Play-off games themselves. Best's season had proved something of disappointment in which he scored just two goals in 19 appearances with seven assists. He fell out with coach Rob Newman and decided to leave The Strikers in late July.

NASL AMERICAN CONFERENCE EASTERN DIVISION

			Shirt	Goals	Score
1. 31st March 1979	New England Tea Men	H	3		2-0
2. 8th April 1979	Toronto Blizzard	A	3		2-1
3. 14th April 1979	Washington Diplomats	H	3		0-4
4. 22nd April 1979	New York Cosmos	A	3		2-3
5. 28th April 1979	Tampa Bay Rowdies	H	3		1-2
6. 5th May 1979	Philadelphia Fury	A	3		1-2
7. 12th May 1979	Toronto Blizzard	H	3		4-0
8. 26th May 1979	Memphis Rogues	H	3		3-1
9. 16th June 1979	San Jose Earthquakes	H	3		3-1
10. 20th June 1979	Tulsa Roughnecks	H	3	1	3-2
11. 23rd June 1979	Tampa Bay Rowdies	A	3		2-1
12. 27th June 1979	Detroit Express	A	3		2-8
13. 4th July 1979	Chicago Sting	H	3		2-3
14. 7th July 1979	San Jose Earthquakes	A	3		2-1
15. 11th July 1979	San Diego Sockers	A	3		3-2
16. 14th July 1979	Rochester Lancers	A	3		1-2
17. 18th July 1979	New York Cosmos	H	3		3-4
18. 21st July 1979	Portland Timbers	A	3	1	1-4
19. 25th July 1979	California Surf	A	3		6-3

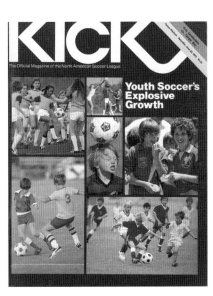

Fort Lauderdale Strikers versus Tulsa Roughnecks, 20th June 1979.

Tampa Bay Rowdies versus Fort Lauderdale Strikers, 23rd June 1979.

Hibernian manager, Eddie Turnbull, flew to London on November 16th 1979 to secure the services of George Best for a fee of £50,000 and reported wages of £2,000 per week. Due to an ankle injury Best did not make his debut for the Hibees until 24th November at St Mirren. A crowd of 13,670 gathered to see George score, though his new team lost the game 2-1. His home debut on 1st December saw Hibernian beat Partick Thistle 2-1. A crowd of 20,622 was present which was an increase of 13,000 compared to their previous home league game. Significantly, it proved to be Hibernian's first victory for 13 league matches. George missed the next game against Morton due to injury but he returned for the visit of Rangers three days before Christmas. Hibernian won the game 2-1.

Best played in a 3-1 defeat at Kilmarnock on 5th January and then scored his second league goal in the 1-1 home draw against Celtic the week after. He then appeared in the Scottish FA Cup 3rd round 1-0 away win against Meadowbank Thistle. George failed to appear for the home game against Morton on 9th February and was suspended by the club. He returned for the 1-0 away defeat at Rangers on 1st March and then figured in a goalless draw the following week against Berwick Rangers in the Scottish Cup Quarter-final. A 3-0 defeat at Dundee followed before George faced the same opposition at home on 25th March. Best's put in a magnificent performance although a crowd of just 5,000 spectators witnessed it. He scored the first goal in a 2-0 win.

Unfortunately, Hibernian's form dipped dramatically after the game and George did not play in a winning side for the remainder of his season. Defeats against Celtic, Dundee United, St Mirren, and a draw at Aberdeen followed. His last game of the season against Dundee United at Easter Road on 19th April also resulted in defeat.

Most disappointingly for Best and Hibernian was their defeat against Celtic in the Scottish Cup Semi-final at Hampden Park on 12th April. An attendance of 32,925 saw Hibernian concede five goals without reply. The Hibees elimination from the competition was coupled with relegation. Best played in 16 competitive games during the season and scored three goals.

Hibernian league debut versus St Mirren, 24th November 1979.

Home league debut versus Partick Thistle, 1st December 1979.

Scottish Cup Semi final versus Celtic at Hampden Park, 12th April 1980.

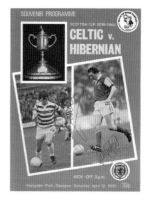

SCOTTISH PREMIER DIVISION

			Shirt	Goals	Score
1. 24th November 1979	St Mirren	A	11	1	1-2
2. 1st December 1979	Partick Thistle	H	11		2-1
3. 22nd December 1979	Rangers	H	11		2-1
4. 5th January 1980	Kilmarnock	A	11		1-3
5. 12th January 1980	Celtic	H	11	1	1-1
6. 1st March 1980	Rangers	A	11		0-1
7. 15th March 1980	Dundee	A	11		0-3
8. 25th March 1980	Dundee	H	11	1	2-0
9. 29th March 1980	Celtic	A	11		0-4
10. 2nd April 1980	Dundee United	H	11		0-2
11. 5th April 1980	St Mirren	A	11		0-2
12. 16th April 1980	Aberdeen	A	11		1-1
13. 19th April 1980	Dundee United	H	11		0-2

SCOTTISH FA CUP

			Shirt	Goals	Score
1. 26th January 1980 Round 3	Meadowbank Thistle	N	11		1-0
2. 8th March 1980 Quarter-final	Berwick Rangers	A	11		0-0
3. 12th April 1980 Semi-final	Celtic	N	11		0-5

FRIENDLIES

			Shirt	Goals	Score
1. 8th December 1979	Kilmarnock	A	11		0-4
2. 10th December 1979	Leicester City	H	11		3-2
3. 15th January 1980	Leicester City	A	11		2-0

In April 1980 George Best returned to Florida and signed to play soccer at the Spartan Stadium, the home of the San Jose Earthquakes. His new side were coached by Bill Foulkes a former team mate at Manchester United. George played his first game of the season on 27th April at Edmonton Drillers though his new team lost 4-2. The Earthquakes were three games into a six game losing run and did not record their first victory of the season until they defeated Edmonton Drillers 1-0 at home on 15th May. A resounding 3-0 home win followed two days later against Houston Hurricane before the next six games saw three wins and three defeats.

George failed to score in his first nine games before he scored in a 2-1 home win against Philadelphia Fury on 14th June. The Earthquakes lost their next three games though Best was on the score sheet George at Washington Diplomats on 22nd June though his side were defeated 5-4. The team won one of their next five games with Best scoring in a 5-1 home win against California Surf on 29th June. A further 2-1 away win followed against Atlanta Chiefs on 12th July Four further defeats followed before The Earthquakes won two of their remaining six games of the season. Best scored in a defeat at Chicago Sting, netted two in the loss against Portland Timbers and scored in the defeat at Los Angeles Aztecs. He also scored in a 3-2 win at San Diego Sockers on 20th August.

Best's first season at San Jose Earthquakes proved a disappointment. While he scored eight goals in 26 appearances with 11 assists, his side lost 23 of their 32 matches. The Earthquakes finished bottom of the Western Division of the American Conference with the fewest points total of any of the 24 teams in the NASL.

Portland Timbers Versus San Jose Earthquakes, 24th May 1980.

San Jose Earthquakes versus Dallas Tornado, 2nd July 1980.

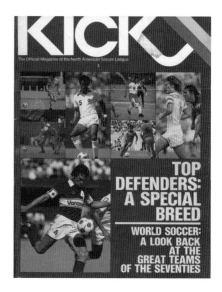

NASL AMERICAN CONFERENCE WESTERN DIVISION

			Shirt	Goals	Score
1. 27th April 1980	Edmonton Drillers	A	11		2-4
2. 30th April 1980	San Diego Sockers	H	11		2-3
3. 3rd May 1980	Seattle Sounders	A	11		0-4
4. 10th May 1980	New England Tea Men	H	11		0-1
5. 15th May 1980	Edmonton Drillers	H	11		1-0
6. 17th May 1980	Houston Hurricane	H	11		3-0
7. 24th May 1980	Portland Timbers	A	11		1-2
8. 7th June 1980	Vancouver Whitecaps	H	11		2-0
9. 11th June 1980	Detroit Express	A	11		1-0
10. 14th June 1980	Philadelphia Fury	H	11	1	2-1
11. 17th June 1980	Fort Lauderdale Strikers	A	11		0-4
12. 22nd June 1980	Washington Diplomats	A	11	1	4-5
13. 26th June 1980	Toronto Blizzard	A	11		2-3
14. 29th June 1980	California Surf	H	11	1	5-1
15. 2nd July 1980	Dallas Tornado	H	11		1-2
16. 5th July 1980	New England Tea Men	A	11		1-3
17. 9th July 1980	Tampa Bay Rowdies	A	11		1-4
18. 12th July 1980	Atlanta Chiefs	A	11		2-1
19. 16th July 1980	Tampa Bay Rowdies	H	11		0-3
20. 19th July 1980	Vancouver Whitecaps	A	11		1-4
21. 30th July 1980	Memphis Rogues	H	11		0-1
22. 9th August 1980	Chicago Sting	A	11	1	1-4
23. 12th August 1980	Memphis Rogues	A	11		0-1
24. 16th August 1980	Portland Timbers	H	11	2	2-3
25. 20th August 1980	San Diego Sockers	A	11	1	3-2
26. 23rd August 1980	Los Angeles Aztecs	H	11	1	1-2

First game of the new season versus Dundee, 9th September 1980.

Appearance versus Dunfermline Athletic, 4th October 1980.

Opposite. Appearance versus Ayr United, (League Cup, Quarter-final, 1st leg), 8th October 1980.

Opposite. Final appearance for Hibernian versus Falkirk, 11th October 1980.

George Best returned to Hibernian for the 1980 / 1981 season after their relegation from the Scottish Premier League. His return though was brief and incorporated just six appearances. His first appearance was at Dundee on 9th September which saw The Hibees win 2-1. Best appeared again the following week in a 1-1 draw at Hamilton Academical. Attention was switched to the Scottish League Cup on 24th September when Best and his team won their League Cup 3rd round 2nd leg tie 2-1 against Clyde. George then appeared in the Scottish league game at Dunfermline Athletic on 4th October which resulted in a 2-0 win for Hibernian. A further appearance in the League Cup Quarter-final 1st leg followed on 8th October at Ayr United. George played the game in borrowed boots after his own had gone missing and helped his side to a 2-2 draw.

George's season was concluded on 11th October when he played in the home game against Falkirk. It ended on a bright note as Hibernian won the game 2-0 in front of 6,947 supporters. George had played in only 22 games for Hibernian in fragmented parts of two seasons but his appearances generated considerable interest in Scotland. He returned to California leaving Hibernian to enjoy a successful campaign which saw them return to the Scottish Premier League as Champions after just one season.

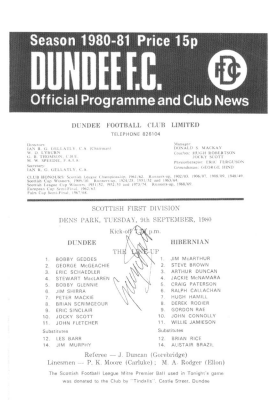

SCOTTISH DIVISION 1

			Shirt	Goals	Score
1. 9th September 1980	Dundee	A	11		2-1
2. 20th September 1980	Hamilton Academical	A	11		1-1
3. 4th October 1980	Dunfermline Athletic	A	11		2-0
4. 11th October 1980	Falkirk	H	11		2-0

BELL'S LEAGUE CUP

			Shirt	Goals	Score
1. 24th September 1980 Round 3 2nd leg	Clyde	H	11		2-1
2. 8th October 1980 Quarter-final 1st leg	Ayr United	A	11		2-2

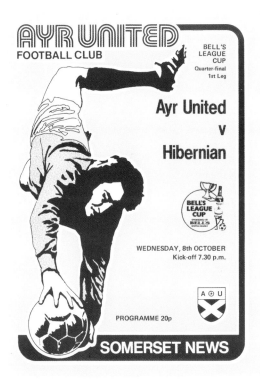

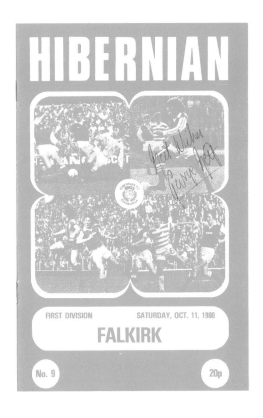

NASL INDOOR LEAGUE				Shirt	Goals	Score
1. 14th November 1980	Los Angeles Aztecs	H		11	2	5-4
2. 21st November 1980	San Diego Sockers	A		11	2	6-4
3. 29th November 1980	Seattle Sounders	A		11	2	5-9
4. 5th December 1980	Los Angeles Aztecs	H		11	3	7-10
5. 12th December 1980	Tulsa Roughnecks	H		11	2	10-8
6. 20th December 1980	Tulsa Roughnecks	A		11	1	8-6
7. 23rd December 1980	San Diego Sockers	H		11	3	13-6
8. 4th January 1981	Portland Timbers	H		11	1	6-2
9. 9th January 1981	California Surf	H		11	4	8-4
10. 18th January 1981	California Surf	A		11	1	8-5
11. 23rd January 1981	Seattle Sounders	H		11	1	8-9
12. 7th February 1981	Dallas Tornado	H		11	1	6-9

SAN JOSE EARTHQUAKES 1981

Best played in The Earthquakes first game of the season at home to New York Cosmos on 29th March in front of their biggest crowd of the season. An attendance of 20,671 spectators saw The Cosmos win the game 3-0. George did not score until the fourth game of the season in a 2-1 home win against San Diego Sockers. He then scored in the return fixture, though the Earthquakes lost 4-2. He scored again three games later in a 2-1 away win against California Surf. Two away losses and a home win followed before George netted two goals against Calgary Boomers on on 31st May. The match finished 4-3 to The Earthquakes though Best had to wait another three games before he scored in a 3-1 home win against Atlanta Chiefs. A run of eight consecutive defeats followed with the Irishman contributing goals at home to Los Angeles Aztecs and away to Tampa Bay Rowdies and Jacksonsville Tea Men.

San Jose's next win did not come until they beat Fort Lauderdale Strikers at home on 22nd July. Best's side won the game 3-2 and he contributed two goals. One of his efforts was deemed one of his finest ever goals when he weaved his way through the The Strikers back line before firing home. Three days later The Earthquakes were defeated at Los Angeles Aztecs 3-0. On 1st August George converted in a 2-1 home loss to Portland Timbers. Four days later the team lost 3-0 away to San Diego Sockers.

Best missed successive wins against Seattle Sounders at home and California Surf away before scoring his last ever goal in the NASL in the penultimate game of the season. George scored in a 3-2 home defeat by San Diego Sockers on 15th August. His final appearance came four days later when San Jose were beaten 3-1 away to Vancouver Whitecaps. George missed only two matches all season. He played in 30 games and scored 13 goals with 10 assists. San Jose Earthquakes again finished bottom of the Western Division though George's career in the North American Soccer League was rapidly drawing to a conclusion.

NASL WESTERN DIVISION

			Shirt	Goals	Score
1. 29th March 1981	New York Cosmos	H	11		0-3
2. 5th April 1981	Los Angeles Aztecs	A	11		0-1
3. 12th April 1981	Jacksonville Tea Men	H	11		3-0
4. 19th April 1981	San Diego Sockers	H	11	1	2-1
5. 26th April 1981	California Surf	H	11		0-1
6. 2nd May 1981	San Diego Sockers	A	11	1	2-4
7. 6th May 1981	Portland Timbers	A	11		0-3
8 10th May 1981	Edmonton Drillers	H	11		1-0
9. 15th May 1981	California Surf	A	11	1	2-1
10 19th May 1981	Atlanta Chiefs	A	11		0-2
11. 24th May 1981	Calgary Boomers	A	11		0-1
12. 27th May 1981	Los Angeles Aztecs	H	11		3-2
13. 31st May 1981	Calgary Boomers	H	11	2	4-3
14. 7th June 1981	Tampa Bay Rowdies	H	11		2-1
15. 14th June 1981	Edmonton Drillers	A	11		2-6
16. 17th June 1981	Atlanta Chiefs	H	11	1	3-1
17. 20th June 1981	Seattle Sounders	A	11		0-1
18. 24th June 1981	California Surf	A	11		0-7
19. 27th June 1981	Los Angeles Aztecs	H	11	1	1-2
20. 1st July 1981	Vancouver Whitecaps	H	11		1-5
21. 4th July 1981	Fort Lauderdale Strikers	A	11		1-4
22. 8th July 1981	Tampa Bay Rowdies	A	11	1	2-4
23. 11th July 1981	Jacksonville Tea Men	A	11	1	3-4
24. 15th July 1981	Montreal Manic	A	11		0-4
25. 22nd July 1981	Fort Lauderdale Strikers	H	11	2	3-2
26. 25th July 1981	Los Angeles Aztecs	A	11		0-3
27. 1st August 1981	Portland Timbers	H	11	1	1-2
28. 5th August 1981	San Diego Sockers	A	11		0-3
29. 15th August 1981	San Diego Sockers	H	11	1	2-3
30. 19th August 1981	Vancouver Whitecaps	A	11		1-3

San Jose Earthquakes versus Vancouver Whitecaps, 1st July 1981.

Final appearance in the North American Soccer League. Vancouver Whitecaps versus San Jose Earthquakes, 19th August 1981.

George neared completion of his career with The Earthquakes following a week long tour to Britain. He featured in all four of the team's games though failed to score. His first game was a 3-1 defeat at his old club Hibernian on 5th October followed two days later by a 1-1 draw at Linfield. San Jose were then defeated 5-2 at Motherwell. The next day the team travelled to Brentford where they were thrashed 8-2. The Earthquakes had been scheduled to complete their short tour at Exeter City on 13th October but the American side pulled out of the game just hours before kick off.

At the conclusion of the tour, George declared that he had to decide where his future lay. He added that he had his family to think of. Prior to the tour Manchester United had shown interest in re-signing Best and during it Middlesbrough were also interested. Despite approaches from both English clubs, Best turned down their advances and returned to San Jose. His NASL career ended after playing five indoor league games of the 1981 / 82 season.

British Tour versus Hibernian, 5th October 1981.

British Tour versus Linfield, 7th October 1981.

British Tour versus Motherwell, 11th October 1981.

British Tour versus Brentford, 12th October 1981.

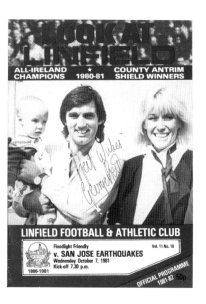

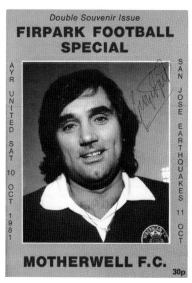

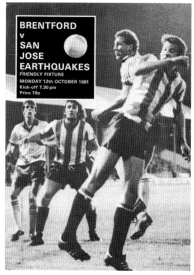

BRITISH TOUR					
			Shirt	Goals	Score
1. 5th October 1981	Hibernian	A	11		1-3
2. 7th October 1981	Linfield	A	11		1-1
3. 11th October 1981	Motherwell	A	11		2-5
4. 12th October 1981	Brentford	A	11		2-8

NASL INDOOR LEAGUE					
			Shirt	Goals	Score
1. 6th December 1981	Seattle Sounders	H	11		7-6
2. 18th December 1981	San Diego Sockers	H	11	5	10-9
3. 20th December 1981	Edmonton Drillers	H	11	2	8-7
4. 6th January 1982	Seattle Sounders	H	11	1	5-2
5.					

FRIENDLIES 1981 / 82

Jim Platt Testimonial. Appearance for Middlesbrough versus Sunderland, 8th September 1981.

Appearance for Annagh United versus Oxford United, 28th May 1982.

George Best signed for AFC Bournemouth on 24th March 1983 and made his debut two days later in a home game against Newport County. The Cherries were 14th in the Third Division but a heavier George still created considerable interest among the Bournemouth public. A crowd of over 9,121 attended the match which saw George play in an unfamiliar role at centre-forward though he failed to score as his latest side lost 1-0.

A 2-1 home win to Chesterfield and a goalless draw at Southend United were followed by a 1-0 home victory against Lincoln City. George's career in English league football was concluded on 7th May in a home game against Wigan Athletic. A crowd of 4,523 watched Best play his part in a 2-2 draw. George was just 15 days short of his 37th Birthday and while he had not managed to score in any of his five appearances he did boost attendances. Bournemouth finished the season in 14th place while Best's competitive playing career was almost at its end.

*Debut for AFC
Bournemouth versus
Newport County, 26th
March 1983.*

*Paul Christopher & Cyril
Smith Testimonial, 25th
April 1983.*

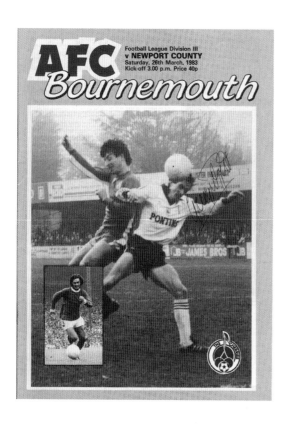

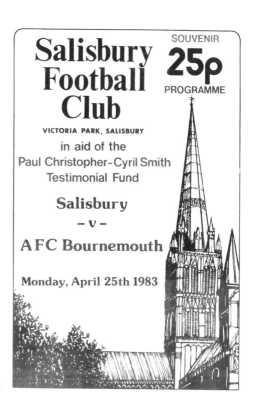

LEAGUE DIVISION 3			Shirt	Goals	Score
1. 26th March 1983	Newport County	H	7		0-1
2. 9th April 1983	Chesterfield	H	7		2-1
3. 16th April 1983	Southend United	A	7		0-0
4. 23rd April 1983	Lincoln City	H	7		1-0
5. 7th May 1983	Wigan Athletic	H	7		2-2

FRIENDLY			Shirt	Goals	Score
1. 25th April 1983 Paul Christopher-Cyril Smith Testimonial Fund	Salisbury	A	7		2-0

Poster displayed on turnstile doors notifying of non-appearance either versus Orient (2nd April 1983) or Doncaster Rovers (2nd May 1983).

Final appearance for AFC Bournemouth versus Wigan Athletic, 7th May 1983.

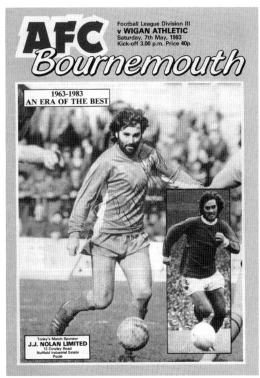

George Best was five weeks beyond his 37th Birthday when he signed a three week contract to play for Brisbane Lions early in July 1983. His first match for the Australian Club came against Sydney Olympic at home on 3rd July. While George had a reasonably quite first half touching the ball only 16 times his presence inspired his team mates. Watched by a disappointing crowd of only 3,000 The Lions trailed to a 31st minute goal but levelled just before the break from a free kick which was awarded after Best was fouled outside the penalty box. Victory came in the 88th minute as The Lions won the game 2-1.

On the 8th July Best lined up to play in a home game against St George Budapest. It proved an unhappy occasion as his team lost 3-0 His next appearance came two days later in an away game at Marconi. His performance was lacklustre in his only game for the Lions in Sydney. While Best's passing was good he looked sluggish and his performance was again below par. Some 3,000 spectators turned up to watch Best's third game end in a 1-1 draw.

George's final appearance for Brisbane Lions was on the 17th July 1983 in a home match against Adelaide City Juventus which proved another unhappy experience as his team crashed 4-0 It was reported that George spent large parts of the game walking around the pitch showing limited interest and contributing little to the team. It was an unhappy way for George to end his brief time in Brisbane. Sadly, only 1,600 spectators witnessed his finale.

NATIONAL SOCCER LEAGUE OF AUSTRALIA					
			Shirt	Goals	Score
1. 3rd July 1983	Sydney Olympic	H	7		2-1
2. 8th July 1983	St. George Budapest	H	7		0-3
3. 10th July 1983	Marconi	A	7		1-1
4. 17th July 1983	Adelaide City Juventus	H	7		0-4

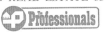

Penultimate appearance versus Marconi, 10th July 1983.

Flyer. 18th July 1983.

Opposite. Certificate from soccer coaching clinic.

George was originally scheduled to appear back in his native Northern Ireland on Saturday 28th January 1984. Unfortunately, due to bad weather which made the pitch unplayable the fixture was put back to Wednesday February 1st. Once again the poor weather meant the game was postponed until Thursday 9th February. George finally played his first and only club game in his home country in front of approximately 3,500 fans. He was less than four months from his 38th Birthday when he pulled on the Tobermore United shirt for their Bass Irish Cup 1st Round tie against Ballymena United. It proved an unhappy occasion both for George and his south Londonderry side as their opponents ran out 7-0 winners. George's involvement in the game was minimal and the closest he came to scoring was a long range effort in the closing minutes which went wide of the post. The game proved to be Best's last competitive match in football.

BASS IRISH CUP, FIRST ROUND					
			Shirt	Goals	Score
1. 9th February 1984	Ballymena United	H	7		0-7

Only appearance in Irish League versus Ballymena United (Irish Cup Round 1), 9th February 1984.

Daily Express Championship, 4th November 1970.

Daily Express Championship, 7th November 1973.

Daily Express Championship, 3th November 1976.

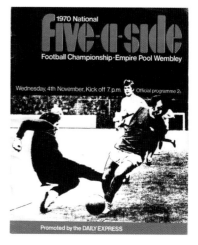

The popular tournament began in 1968 though Manchester United did not enter for the first two years. In 1970 they entered for the first time and Best was in scintillating form scoring five goals as United won the trophy. The following year George was withdrawn from the competition only minutes before it was due to start. He was not part of the team which entered in 1972 but returned for the tournament in 1973. United reached the Quarter-finals but were eliminated by tournament winners Derby County. Best made his final appearance in the tournament when he represented Fulham in 1976 but after reaching the second round they were defeated by Tottenham Hotspur.

MANCHESTER UNITED		Shirt	Goals	Score
1. 4th November 1970 Round 1 Won 4-3 on penalties	Celtic	6	1	1-1
2. 4th November 1970 Round 2 Won 6-5 on penalties	Ipswich Town	6		1-1
3. 4th November 1970 Semi-finals	Crystal Palace	6	2	3-0
4. 4th November 1970 Final	Tottenham Hotspur	6	2	2-1

		Shirt	Goals	Score
1. 7th November 1973 Round 1	Middlesbrough	5		1-0
2. 7th November 1973 Quarter-final	Derby County	5		0-2

FULHAM		Shirt	Goals	Score
1. 3rd November 1976 Round 1	Coventry City	4		1-0
2. 3rd November 1976 Round 2	Tottenham Hotspur	4		0-3

Appearance for Ballymoney Invitation XI versus North-West Select, 3rd July 1984.

Jackie McNamara Testimonial. Appearance for Hibernian versus Newcastle United, 5th August 1984.

Appearance for Jamie's All Stars versus The Dennis Waterman XI, 14th October 1984.

Appearance for Reading versus New Zealand, 29th October 1984.

Opposite. Appearance for George Best 'All Stars' Versus Lawbreakers XI, 2nd February 1986.

Opposite. George Dunlop Testimonial. Appearance for George Best's All Stars versus Linfield, 17th February 1986.

Opposite. Appearance for George Best XI versus Maidstone United, 6th April 1986.

Opposite. Appearance for Workington versus Lancashire Football League XI, 9th April 1986.

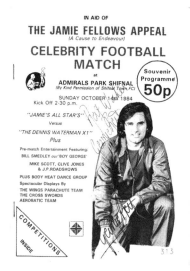

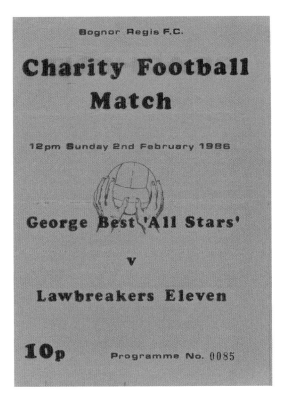

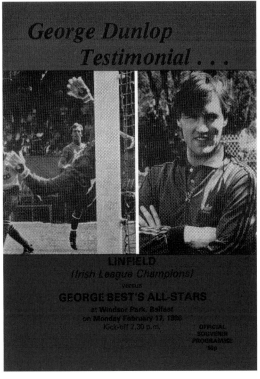

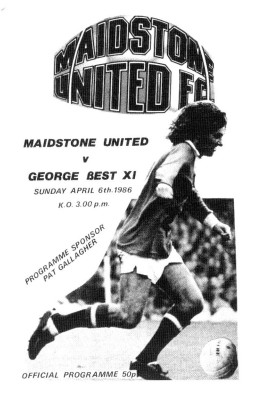

Tony Currie Testimonial,
5th October 1986.

Pat Jennings Testimonial,
3rd December 1986.

Tommy Tuite Testimonial,
10th March 1987

Appearance for Star
Select Team versus
Hanover Select Team,
1st May 1988.

Appearance for The
George Best Newhaven
Select XI versus TV
Entertainers XI, 8th
May 1988

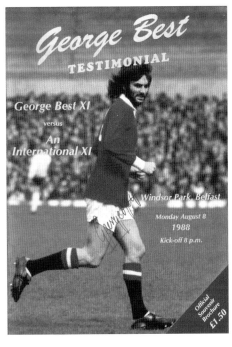

George Best Testimonial poster.

George Best Testimonial, 8th August 1988.

Match ticket for the George Best Testimonial.

FRIENDLIES 1989 / 90

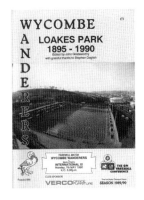

Appearance for Panini International Allstars versus Arsenal / Spurs Select, 24th September 1989.

Appearance for Crewe United versus Dundalk, 5th December 1989.

Appearance for Martin O'Neill's International XI versus Wycombe Wanderers, 7th May 1990.

28th July 1969 Prince of Wales Investiture	Wales v **Rest of the United Kingdom** at Cardif City FC	0-1
16th November 1969 Underprivileged Childrens' Toy Fund	**Blinkers United** v All Stars XI at Belle Vue, Manchester	7-2
27th January 1971 Lord Provost's Disaster fund	Scotland XI v **Rangers Celtic Select** at Queens Park FC	2-1
1st May 1972 Uwe Seeler Farewell	Hamburg SV v **World Team XI**	3-7
25th September 1973 Eusebio Testimonial	Benfica v **Rest of the World**	2-2
5th August 1974 Friendly	**Dunstable Town** v Manchester United	3-2
12th August 1974 Friendly	**Dunstable Town** v Cork Celtic	0-0
29th October 1974 Jeff Astle Testimonial	**West Bromwich Albion '68** v West Bromwich Albion '74	2-1
27th November 1974 Tony Book Testimonial	Manchester City XI v **All Stars XI**	4-6
2nd September 1975 Mike Summerbee Testimonial	Manchester City XI v **Manchester United EC Winners' XI**	3-4
29th October 1975 Friendly	**Dunstable Town** v Luton Town	1-1

18th November 1975 Paul Aimson Testimonial	Bury v **All Stars XI**	3-2
24th November 1975 Peter Osgood Testimonial	**Chelsea Past** v Chelsea Present	3-4
26th November 1975 Pat Crerand Testimonial	Manchester United v **European Cup Winners' 1968**	7-2
20th October 1976 Mike Bailey Testimonial	**Wolverhampton Wanderers** v West Bromwich Albion	3-0
September 1978 Friendly	FC Lask v **Detroit Express**	2-2
13th November 1979 Bobby Robson Testimonial	**Ipswich Town** v England	2-2

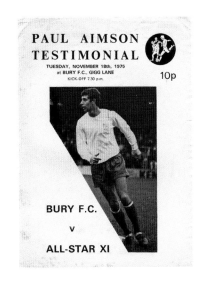

Opposite. Appearance for Rest of the United Kingdom versus Wales, 28th July 1969.

Opposite. Appearance for Rangers / Celtic XI Versus Scotland XI, 27th January 1971.

Opposite. Uwe Seller Farewell. Appearance for World Team XI versus Hamburg SV, 1st May 1972.

Paul Aimson Testimonial. Appearance for All Star XI versus Bury, 18th November 1975.

Match ticket for Mike Bailey Testimonial, 20th October 1976.

Mike Bailey Testimonial. Appearance for Wolverhampton Wanderers versus West Bromwich Albion, 20th October 1976.

Bobby Robson Testimonial. Appearance for Ipswich Town versus England, 13th November 1979.

26th November 1979 Gareth Davis Testimonial	**Wrexham** v Wolverhampton Wanderers	3-2
3rd December 1979 David Nish Testimonial	Derby County v **Derby County Championship Select XI**	1-3
8th September 1981 Jim Platt Testimonial	**Middlesbrough** v Sunderland	1-2
21st October 1981 Friendly	**Portadown** v **Glenavon**	1-0
28th May 1982 Friendly	**Annagh United** v Oxford United	1-2
4th August 1982 Friendly	**Valur** v Manchester United	1-5
5th August 1982 Friendly	**KA Akureyri** v Manchester United	1-7
7th August 1982 Friendly	**Scone Thistle** v Scone Amateurs	

Gareth Davis Testimonial. Appearance for Wrexham versus Wolverhampton Wanderers, 26th November 1979.

David Nish Testimonial. Appearance for Derby County Championship Select XI versus Derby County, 3rd December 1979.

Opposite. Appearance for Arbroath Victoria versus Arbroath, 8th August 1982.

Opposite. Appearance for Glentoran versus Manchester United, 14th August 1982.

Opposite. Appearance for Ian Botham's All Star Saab XI versus Scunthorpe United, 21st September 1982.

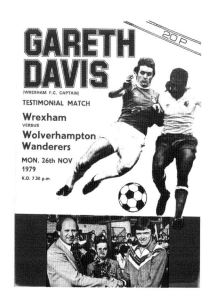

8th August 1982 Friendly	**Arbroath Victoria** v Arbroath	4-3
14th August 1982 Centenary	**Glentoran** v Manchester United	0-2
23rd August 1982 Chris Garland Benefit	Bristol City v **All Star XI**	4-3
5th September 1982 Sick Childrens hospital, Yorkhill, Glasgow	Personalities XI v **Stable Bar All Stars** at Pollock Juniors FC	4-11
21st September 1982 Friendly	Scunthorpe United v **Ian Botham All Star Saab XI**	0-2
27th September 1982 Friendly	**Bangor** v Motherwell	1-5
28th September 1982 Friendly	**Ballymena United** v Motherwell	2-1
8th October 1982 Hong Kong League First Division	**Sea Bee** v Bulova	3-5
17th October 1982 Hong Kong League First Division	**Sea Bee** v Ting Sing	2-4
19th October 1982 Peter Nicholson Testimonial	**Peter Nicholson's '78 XI** v Bolton Wanderers 1982 / 83 at Bolton Wanderers FC	0-4
14th November 1982 Hong Kong League First Division	**Hong Kong Rangers** v Bulova	0-0
22nd November 1982 Hong Kong League First Division	**Hong Kong Rangers** v Seiko	0-1

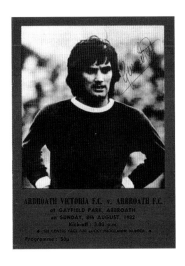

28th November 1982 Soccer Celebrity Special	**George Best All Stars** v Jim Davidson XI at Plymouth Argyle FC	11-8
12th December 1982 Charity	Barnstaple Town v **George Best All stars**	1-4
19th January 1983 Exhibition	Falmouth Town v **Penryn Athletic**	6-1
27th February 1983 Fund Raising	**Chairman's XI** v Lytham at Lytham FC	2-2
7th March 1983 Friendly	**Nuneaton Borough** v Coventry City	2-1
27th March 1983 Survival Special	A Bridgewater Town XI v **George Best All Star XI**	2-5
24th April 1983 Graham Brooking fundraiser	**Star Rider XI** v Foxhall United at Torquay United FC	3-5
24th May 1983 Ballyclare May Festival Week	**Ballyclare Comrades** v Glentoran	1-1
24th July 1983 Friendly	**Osborne Park Galeb** v Melville Alemannia	2-1

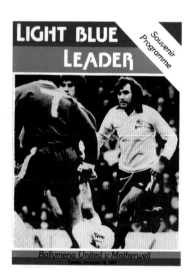

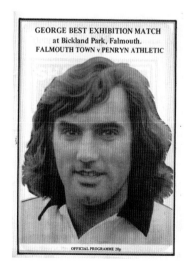

July 1983 Plaza Ceramics Cup	**West Adelaide** v Adelaide City	5-3
12th August 1983 Friendly	**Newry Town** v Shamrock Rovers	3-3
10th October 1983 Peter Dornan Testimonial	**Linfield** v Everton	0-5
19th January 1984 Friendly	Bahrain v **UK XI**	
21st January 1984 Friendly	Dubai XI v **UK XI**	
4th March 1984 In aid of victims of Harrod's bomb blast	**Malcolm MacDonald XI** v Dennis Waterman XI at Fulham FC	9-3
12th May 1984 10th Anniversary Re-union	Golden Bay Earthquakes v **Quakes Alumni**	5-2
16th May 1984 Les Berry Testimonial	**Charlton Athletic** v Arsenal	3-4
20th May 1984 Barry Fry Testimonial	**Barnet** v Tottenham Hotspur	3-6
21st May 1984 Charity	Fivemiletown Select v **Entertainer's XI**	1-2
28th May 1984 In aid of Ballyclare Beacon House Club	**George Best XI** v Billy Neill XI at Ballyclare Comrades FC	0-3

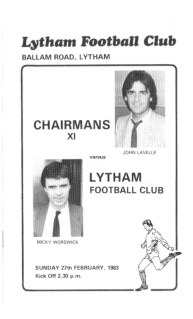

Opposite. Appearance for Ballymena United versus Motherwell, 28th September 1982.

Opposite. Appearance for George Best Allstars versus Barnstaple Town, 12th December 1982.

Opposite. Appearance for Penryn Athletic versus Falmouth Town, 19th January 1983.

Appearance for Chairmans XI versus Lytham, 27th February 1983.

Appearance for Nuneaton Borough versus Coventry City, 7th March 1983.

Date / Event	Match	Score
3rd July 1984 Exhibition	**Ballymoney Invitation XI** v North-West Select at Ballymoney	5-1
27th July 1984 Charity	**George Best XI** v Northern Radio & Press Select at Dingwall	5-1
29th July 1984 Charity	**George Best XI** v Skean Dhu & Northsouth Select at Stonehaven	
5th August 1984 Jackie McNamara Testimonial	**Hibernian** v Newcastle United	0-3
14th August 1984 Jamie Fellows Appeal	**Jamie's All Stars** v The Dennis Waterman XI at Shifnal Town FC	8-4
29th October 1984 Friendly	**Reading** v New Zealand	1-2
5th May 1985 Derek Hales Benefit	**Derek Hales XI** v Football Commentators XI at Welling United FC	5-5
14th May 1985 Peter Foley Testimonial	Oxford United v **Manchester United XI**	1-1
17th May 1985 Bradford City Disaster Appeal	**Aston Villa** v West Bromwich Albion	3-3
1st June 1985 Pre-match entertainment – Freight Rover Trophy	**L.B.C. XI** v England All Stars at Wembley Stadium	1-3
22nd September 1985 In aid of Children's Charity	Kettering Town v **Ron Atkinson's All Stars**	1-3

Appearance for George Best All Star XI versus Bridgewater Town XI, 27th March 1983.

Appearance for Osborne Park Galeb versus Melville Alemannia, 24th July 1983.

Opposite. Peter Dornan Testimonial. Appearance for Linfield versus Everton, 10th October 1983.

Opposite. Appearance for Malcolm MacDonald XI versus Dennis Waterman XI, 4th March 1984.

BRIDGWATER TOWN A.F.C.
SURVIVAL SPECIAL

A BRIDGWATER TOWN XI
v
George Best All Star XI

SUNDAY 17th MARCH 1983

LUCKY NUMBER

No 1131

OFFICIAL PROGRAMME £1.50

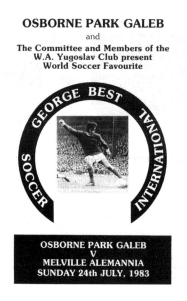

OSBORNE PARK GALEB
and
The Committee and Members of the
W.A. Yugoslav Club present
World Soccer Favourite

GEORGE BEST
INTERNATIONAL
SOCCER

OSBORNE PARK GALEB
V
MELVILLE ALEMANNIA
SUNDAY 24th JULY, 1983

27th October 1985 Friendly	**Ex Tottenham Hotspur** v Norwegian Horribles at Cheshunt	3-2
2nd February 1986 Charity	**George Best's All Stars** v Lawbreakers XI at Bognor Regis FC	3-1
17th February 1986 George Dunlop Testimonial	Linfield v **George Best's All Stars**	6-2
6th April 1986 in aid of 'Read out' Charity	Maidstone United v **George Best XI**	3-4
9th April 1986 Survival Fund Friendly	**Workington** v Lancashire Football League XI	1-1
13th April 1986 Friendly	Ex-AFC Bournemouth XI v **George Best All Stars** at AFC Bournemouth	2-6
28th April 1986 Friendly	Collins Barracks XI v **Liam Tuohy Celebrity XI** at Dublin	**1-2**
24th May 1986 Pre-match entertainment – Freight Rover Trophy	**Mike Morris' TV AM Robins** v Gordon Taylor's PFA Trotters XI at Wembley Stadium	0-0
13th September 1986 Friendly	Germany v **Great Britain**	
5th October 1986 Tony Currie Testimonial	TC's United All Stars v **Dennis Waterman Showbiz XI** at Sheffield United FC	7-5
3rd December 1986 A Tribute to Pat Jennings	**Pat Jennings' Select** v International XI at Linfield FC	3-3

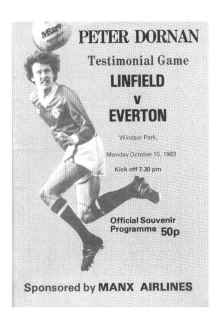

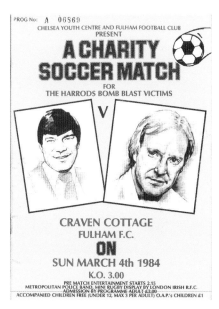

10th March 1987 Tommy Tuite Testimonial	**Epsom & Ewell** v Chelsea FC XI	1-4
22nd April 1988 Kick Aids '88 Charity	Japan Senior All Stars v **Pele All Stars** at Tokyo	0-2
1st May 1988 Charity	**Star Select Team** v Hanover Select Team at Portadown	3-2
8th May 1988 Charity	TV Entertainers XI v **The George Best Newhaven Select XI** at Newhaven FC	1-3
8th August 1988 George Best Testimonial	**George Best XI** v An International XI at Linfield FC	7-6
10th June 1989 15th Anniversary game	**San Jose Earthquakes** v Portland Timbers	1-3
6th July 1989 Charity	Devonport City XI v Tasmania XI	2-2
24th September 1989 Dreamflight Charity Cup	**Panini International All Stars** v Arsenal / Spurs Select at St Albans City FC	5-6
5th December 1989 Friendly	**Crewe United** v Dundalk	1-5
31st January 1990 Friendly	**Wrest Point Hotel Casino XI** v British Airways World XI	

*Les Berry Testimonial.
Appearance for Charlton
Athletic versus Arsenal, 16th
May 1984.*

*Barry Fry Testimonial.
Appearance for Barnet versus
Tottenham Hotspur, 20th
May 1984.*

*Opposite. Appearance for Ron
Atkinson's All Stars versus
Kettering Town, 22nd
September 1985.*

*Opposite. Billy Bingham
Testimonial, Appearance for
Northern Ireland Select versus
Newcastle United, 12th
August 1994.*

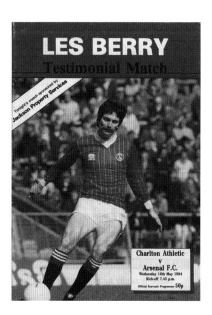

7th May 1990 Farewell to Loakes Park	Wycombe Wanderers v **Martin O'Neill's International XI**	4-8
20th May 1990 Pre-match entertainment Leyland Cup	**Bristol Strollers** v Tranmere Roamers at Wembley Stadium	1-1
11th August 1991 Five-a-side	**Manchester United** v Manchester City Sir Matt Busby Testimonial pre game	3-3
16th October 1991 Opening of floodlights	**Newcastle Town** v Stoke City	2-3
26th July 1992 Chris Garland Benefit	**Minehead Guest XI** v Combined Bristol City, Chelsea & Leicester City Celebrities XI	6-6
28th March 1993 Six-a-side	**The International All Stars** v Old Crystal Palace Malcolm Allison Testimonial pre game	
9th May 1994 Charity	**George Best Ten 17 All Stars** v Rodney Marsh Showbiz XI at Bishop's Storford FC	7-4
12th August 1994 Billy Bingham Testimonial	**Northern Ireland Select** v Newcastle United at Linfield FC	2-5
10th September 1995 Franz Beckenbauer 50th Birthday Celebration	German Select Side v **World XI** at Munich	8-8
19th September 1995 Charity	**Crewe United** v Showbiz Select	6-3

The games listed are confirmed matches in which George Best definitely played. It is not, however, neither a definitive nor an exhaustive list. Additionally, there were other friendly matches in which he was scheduled to appear in but for various reasons did not. **Teams in bold** highlight the side Best appeared for.

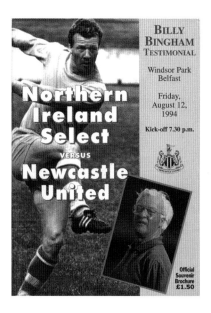

George was not capped at either Northern Ireland schoolboy or Under 23 level though he did make two appearances for his country's youth team. His first appearance came 11 days short of his 17th Birthday when he was part of the side which drew 1-1 against England at Boundary Park, home of Oldham Athletic. Seven days later Best appeared at Park Avenue, home of Aberystwyth Town as his country's youth team again played out a 1-1 draw. George scored Northern Ireland's goal.

YOUTH INTERNATIONALS			Shirt	Goals	Score
1. 11th May 1962	England	A	10		1-1
2. 18th May 1962	Wales	A	10	1	1-1

George Best made his debut for his country on 15th April 1964 a month short of his eighteenth Birthday. The match against Wales in Swansea resulted in a 3-2 win for Northern Ireland. Two weeks later George made his home debut at Windsor Park against Uruguay and was again on the winning side as his country triumphed 3-0. On 3rd October George played in a seven goal thriller as his side lost 4-3 to England. Best played in his first World Cup qualifying game on 14th October 1964 in the 1-0 home win to Switzerland. He scored his first international goal against the same opponents away though his team lost 2-1.

Best inspired Northern Ireland to a 2-1 victory against Holland in a further World qualifying game in Belfast on 17th March 1965 and was also part of the side which gained a goalless draw in Rotterdam in the return fixture on 7th April 1965. He scored again on 7th May in a 4-1 win against Albania in a further World Cup qualifying game in Belfast. Results in the competition though were not sufficient to allow Northern Ireland to compete in the 1966 finals in England.

George made only three appearances for Northern Ireland in each of the years 1966, 1967 and 1968. He scored in the last of these against Turkey in a World Cup qualifier at Windsor Park which Northern Ireland won 4-1. Best played in all three games of the 1969 Home Internationals and against USSR at home in a World Cup qualifier on 10th September 1969. Northern Ireland, though, failed to win any of the quartet of matches. He again faced all three of the home countries in 1970 and while his country lost each game in he scored in the away match against England on 21st April. A European Championship qualifier followed against Spain away on 11th November 1970 but the Irish lost again, 3-0.

Best's appearances for his country in 1971 brought better results. Of the six games he played in that year, Northern Ireland won four of the matches. He scored against Cyprus in a 3-0 win in Nicosia in a European Championship qualifying game on

Opposite. Debut for Northern Ireland Youth versus England, 11th May 1962.

Opposite. Team page England v Northern Ireland.

Debut for Northern Ireland versus Wales, 15th April 1964.

Appearance versus Scotland, 21st October 1967.

3rd February. George then netted his only hat-trick for his country in the return game against Cyprus in Belfast on 21st April as Northern Ireland ran out 5-0 winners. Other Irish victories came that year in the Home Internationals with 1-0 wins against Scotland away and Wales at home. George made two appearances for his country the following year. Due to sectarian troubles in Belfast, Northern Ireland had to play their European Championship qualifying game against Spain in Hull. They drew the match 1-1 and then lost a World Cup qualifier 3-0 in the next game away to Bulgaria.

George's problems at Manchester United began to limit his appearances for his country as he played in just one game in 1973 against Portugal in Lisbon in a World Cup qualifier on 14th November. The game ended in a 1-1 draw but results in the competition were not good enough for Northern Ireland to qualify for the 1974 World Cup finals. George did not play for his country again for another three years when, as a Fulham player, he inspired Northern Ireland to a 2-2 draw against Holland in a World Cup qualifying game in Rotterdam. His next game was in the same competition against Belgium in Liege on 10th November 1976 though Best's country lost 2-0.

George's international career came to an end in 1977 during which he played three final games. He appeared in the 5-0 defeat in West Germany on 27th April and on 21st September he played against Iceland in Belfast in a World Cup qualifying match which the Irish won 2-0. Best made his final appearance for his country in the same competition the following month as Northern Ireland were beaten by Holland 1-0 in Belfast.

It was disappointing that Northern Ireland failed to qualify for the World Cup finals of 1966, 1970 and 1974 nor the European Championships of 1968, 1972 or 1976. Best, for a variety of reasons missed many of the qualifiers in both competitions and was subsequently denied playing in the major finals. His appearances for his country totalled just 37 over a 13 and a half year period.

Hat-trick versus Cyprus, 21 April 1971.

Appearance versus USSR, 22nd September 1971.

Appearance versus Spain, 16th February 1972.

Appearance versus Holland, 13th October 1976.

Appearance versus West Germany, 27th April 1977.

Final appearance versus Holland, 12th October 1977.

INTERNATIONALS				Shirt	Goals	Score
1. 15th April 1964	Wales	A	HIC	7		3-2
2. 29th April 1964	Uruguay	H	FRI	7		3-0
3. 3rd October 1964	England	H	HIC	7		3-4
4. 14th October 1964	Switzerland	H	WCQ	7		1-0
5. 14th November 1964	Switzerland	A	WCQ	7	1	1-2
6. 25th November 1964	Scotland	A	HIC	7		2-3
7. 17th March 1965	Holland	H	WCQ	11		2-1
8. 7th April 1965	Holland	A	WCQ	7		0-0
9. 7th May 1965	Albania	H	WCQ	11	1	4-1
10. 2nd October 1965	Scotland	H	HIC	11		3-2
11. 10th November 1965	England	A	HIC	11		1-2
12. 24th November 1965	Albania	A	WCQ	11		1-1
13. 22nd October 1966	England	H	ENQ	11		0-2
14. 21st October 1967	Scotland	H	HIC	11		1-0
15. 23rd October 1968	Turkey	H	WCQ	11	1	4-1
16. 3rd May 1969	England	H	HIC	11		1-3
17. 6th May 1969	Scotland	A	HIC	7		1-1
18. 10th May 1969	Wales	H	HIC	7		0-0
19. 10th September 1969	USSR	H	WCQ	11		0-0
20. 18th April 1970	Scotland	H	HIC	11		0-1
21. 21st April 1970	England	A	HIC	8	1	1-3
22. 25th April 1970	Wales	A	HIC	8		0-1
23. 11th November 1970	Spain	A	ENQ	8		0-3
24. 3rd February 1971	Cyprus	A	ENQ	11	1	3-0
25. 21st April 1971	Cyprus	H	ENQ	11	3	5-0
26. 15th May 1971	England	H	HIC	11		0-1
27. 18th May 1971	Scotland	A	HIC	11		1-0
28. 22nd May 1971	Wales	H	HIC	11		1-0
29. 22nd September 1971	USSR	A	ENQ	11		0-1
30. 16th February 1972	Spain	N	ENQ	11		1-1
31. 18th October 1972	Bulgaria	A	WCQ	11		0-3
32. 14th November 1973	Portugal	A	WCQ	11		1-1
33 13th October 1976	Holland	A	WCQ	7		2-2
34. 10th November 1976	Belgium	A	WCQ	7		0-2
35. 27th April 1977	West Germany	A	FRI	7		0-5
36. 21st September 1977	Iceland	H	WCQ	10		2-0
37. 12th October 1977	Holland	H	WCQ	10		0-1

Key

WCQ = World Cup Qualifier

ENQ = European Nations Cup Qualifier

HIC = Home (British) International Championship

FRI = Friendly

The George Best Club began in January 1971 and was organised by George's agent, Ken Stanley. The club was set up in the wake of the deluge of fan mail which George would receive. The club operated from small offices in St Georges Square in Huddersfield where George's mail was sorted, sifted and replied to by George with help from Ken and a couple of female assistants.

The club proved amazingly popular. Upon paying a yearly subscription fee of £1 members received a membership wallet, diploma of membership, personal club emblem embroidered in gold thread on black cloth, a detailed-packed personal profile and a giant colour poster of George sitting at the controls of a helicopter. There followed a quarterly club eight page newsletter entitled 'George!'. The content was basic but typically included a one page update from George, black and white photographs, a competition and an occasional letters page from adoring fans. It is not known when either the first or last newsletter was issued or how many there were but seven issues are certainly known to exist.

The George Best Club continued during George's troubled times at Old Trafford and ran for almost twelve months after he had left Manchester United. It finally folded in December 1974. Items from the club remain much sought after and highly collectable.

Newsletter from August 1971.

Opposite. Newsletter from November 1972.

Opposite. Membership certificate.

Opposite. Cloth badge received upon joining The George Best Club.

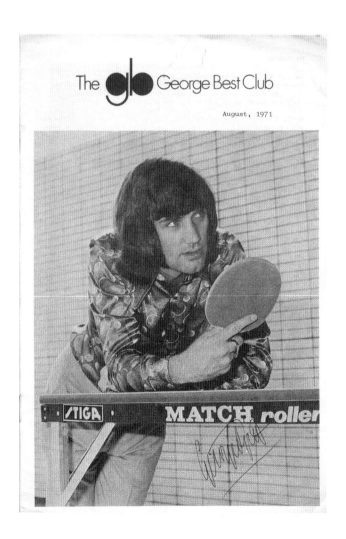

NOVEMBER, 1972

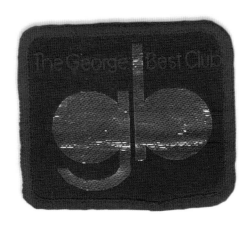

Born in Belfast, 22nd May 1946.

Died in London, 25th November 2005.

Buried in Belfast, 3rd December 2005.

- Won a European Champions Clubs' Cup winners' medal in 1967 / 68.
- Won League Championship winners' medals in 1964 / 65 and 1966 / 67.
- Won a FA Youth Cup winners' medal in 1963 / 64.
- Named British Footballer of the year in 1968.
- Named European Footballer of the year in 1968.
- Won 37 caps for Northern Ireland.
- Won 2 youth caps for Northern Ireland.
- Scored his first league goal in his second league game.
- Scored his first FA Cup goal in his third FA Cup game.
- Scored his first League Cup goal in his third League Cup game.
- Scored his first European goal in his fourth European game.
- Scored his first International goal in his fifth International game.
- Played on 58 of a possible 96 English football league grounds between 1963 / 64 and 1982 / 83.
- In April 1964 played in 11 games including four within six days: *25th April Manchester United v Nottingham Forest (3-1). 27th April Swindon Town Youth v Manchester United Youth (1-1). 29th April Northern Ireland v Uruguay (3-0). 30th April Manchester United Youth v Swindon Town Youth (4-1).*
- In September 1977 played games in Northern Ireland, Wales and Scotland within six days: *21st September Northern Ireland v Iceland (2-0). 24th September Cardiff City v Fulham (3-1). 26th September St Mirren v Fulham (5-3).*
- Played in two FA Charity Shield finals and wasn't on a winning side.
- Never played in a FA Cup final but played in six Semi-finals.
- Never played in a League Cup final but played in four Semi-finals.
- Scored 10 penalties in competitive games for Manchester United.
- Never scored a penalty in a FA Cup game.
- Never scored any penalties for Stockport County, Fulham, Hibernian or AFC Bournemouth in competitive games.
- Only player to be Manchester United's top league scorer for five seasons in succession: *1967 / 68 = 28 goals, 1968 / 69 = 19 goals, 1969 / 70 = 15 goals, 1970 / 71 = 18 goals, 1971 / 72 = 18 goals.*

- Played two games on his Birthday: *22nd May 1971 (25th) Northern Ireland v Wales (1-0). 22nd May 1977 (31st) Los Angeles Aztecs v Vancouver Whitecaps (3-1).*
- Played three times at Wembley: *10th November 1965 England v Northern Ireland (2-1). 29th May 1968 Manchester United v Benfica (4-1). 21st April 1970 England v Northern Ireland (3-1).*
- George Best and Rodney Marsh played in the same Fulham team in 20 competitive games: *(League = 15, FA Cup = 2, League Cup = 3).*
- George Best and Peter Cormack played in the same Hibernian team in eight competitive games: *(League = 7, Scottish FA Cup = 1).*
- His preferred training number at Manchester United was 33 and at Fulham it was 27.
- Played against Manchester United on four occasions: *5th August 1974 Dunstable Town v Manchester United (3-2). 4th August 1982 Valur v Manchester United (1-5). 5th August 1982 KA Akureyri v Manchester United (1-7). 14th August 1982 Glentoran v Manchester United (0-2).*
- Played against Bobby Charlton on five occasions: *3rd October 1964 Northern Ireland v England (3-4). 10th November 1965 England v Northern Ireland (2-1). 22nd October 1966 Northern Ireland v England (0-2). 3rd May 1969 Northern Ireland v England (1-3). 21st April 1970 England v Northern Ireland (3-1).*
- Played against Denis Law on four occasions: *25th November 1964 Scotland v Northern Ireland (3-2). 2nd October 1965 Northern Ireland v Scotland (3-2). 21st October 1967 Northern Ireland v Scotland (1-0). 6th May 1969 Scotland v Northern Ireland (1-1).*

Contrary to popular belief, George scored eight and not nine goals for Northern Ireland. While record books show he scored against Scotland on 25th November 1964, this information is incorrect. George's inaccurate shot in the fog at Hampden Park was met firmly by the head of team mate Willie Irvine and a goal resulted. The newspaper reports and Willie himself confirmed it was not Best's goal. It is not known how the error happened and George seemingly had no desire to correct it.

Picked in a Northern Ireland squad of 22 for the final time for a World Cup Qualifying game against Scotland in Belfast on 14th October 1981. Best though was omitted for the final squad of 17 selected for the match.

HAT-TRICKS

1. **9th March 1963**. Manchester City B v Manchester United B (Lancashire League Division 2) – 4 goals.

2. **30th November 1963**. Burnley A v Manchester United A (Lancashire League Division 1) – 3 goals.

3. **18th December 1963**. Manchester United v Barrow (FA Youth Cup Round 2) – 3 goals.

4. **27th June 1967**. Western Australia v Manchester United (Friendly) – 3 goals.

5. **4th May 1968**. Manchester United v Newcastle United (League Division 1) – 3 goals.

6. **7th February 1970**. Northampton Town v Manchester United (FA Cup Round 5) – 6 goals.

7. **21st April 1971**. Northern Ireland v Cyprus (European Championship Qualifier) – 3 goals.

8. **18th September 1971**. Manchester United v West Ham United (League Division 1) – 3 goals.

9. **27th November 1971**. Southampton v Manchester United (League Division 1) – 3 goals.

10. **18th July 1976**. Los Angeles Aztecs v Boston Minutemen (North American Soccer League Pacific Conference Southern Division) – 3 goals.

NOTABLE SENDING-OFFS

1. **16th October 1968**. Manchester United v Estudiantes (World Club Championship 2nd leg)

2. **18th April 1970**. Northern Ireland v Scotland (Home International Championship)

3. **18th August 1971**. Manchester United v Chelsea (League Division 1)

4. **18th October 1972**. Bulgaria v Northern Ireland (World Cup Qualifier)

5. **2nd October 1976**. Southampton v Fulham (League Division 2)

PENALTIES SCORED

1. **10th December 1966**. Manchester United v Liverpool (League Division 1).

2. **4th May 1968**. Manchester United v Newcastle United (League Division 1) (2).

3. **31st March 1969**. Nottingham Forest v Manchester United (League Division 1).

4. **20th October 1969**. Manchester United v Burnley (League Cup, Round 4, Replay).

5. **3rd February 1971**. Cyprus v Northern Ireland (European Nations Cup Qualifier).

6. **24th April 1971**. Manchester United v Ipswich Town (League Division 1).

7. **15th April 1972**. Manchester United v Southampton (League Division 1).

8. **29th April 1972**. Manchester United v Stoke City (League Division 1).

9. **23rd August 1972**. Manchester United v Leicester City (League Division 1).

10. **12th September** 1972. Manchester United v Oxford United (League Cup, Round 2, Replay).

11. **7th October 1972**. West Bromwich Albion v Manchester United (League Division 1).

APPEARANCES

	A	B	Yth	Res	Lge	Eu	FAC	LC	Tot
Manchester United	20	40	7	9	361	36	46	25	544
Jewish Guild	-	-	-	-	4	-	-	-	4
Stockport County	-	-	-	-	3	-	-	-	3
Cork Celtic	-	-	-	-	3	-	-	-	3
Los Angeles Aztecs	-	-	-	-	61	-	-	-	61
Fulham	-	-	-	1	42	-	2	3	48
Fort Lauderdale Strikers	-	-	-	-	33	-	-	-	33
Hibernian	-	-	-	-	17	-	3	2	22
San Jose Earthquakes	-	-	-	-	56	-	-	-	56
AFC Bournemouth	-	-	-	-	5	-	-	-	5
Brisbane Lions	-	-	-	-	4	-	-	-	4
Tobermore United	-	-	-	-	-	-	1	-	1
Totals	20	40	7	10	589	36	52	30	784

Manchester United	A	B	Yth	Res	Lge	Eu	FAC	LC	Tot
1961 / 62	5	22	-	-	-	-	-	-	27
1962 / 63	10	18	2	-	-	-	-	-	30
1963 / 64	5	-	5	8	17	2	7	-	44
1964 / 65	-	-	-	-	41	11	7	-	59
1965 / 66	-	-	-	-	31	6	5	-	42
1966 / 67	-	-	-	-	42	-	2	1	45
1967 / 68	-	-	-	-	41	9	2	-	52
1968 / 69	-	-	-	-	41	8	6	-	55
1969 / 70	-	-	-	-	37	-	8	8	53
1970 / 71	-	-	-	-	40	-	2	6	48
1971 / 72	-	-	-	-	40	-	7	6	53
1972 / 73	-	-	-	-	19	-	-	4	23
1973 / 74	-	-	-	1	12	-	-	-	13
Totals	20	40	7	9	361	36	46	25	544

Key: A = A Team – Lancashire League Division 1. **B** = B Team – Lancashire League Division 2.
Yth = Youth Team – FA Youth Cup.
Res = Reserve Team – Central League / Football Combination.
Lge = League – Division 1 / R15 000 BP League / Division 4 / Bass League of Ireland / North American Soccer League / Division 2 / Scottish Premier Division / Scottish Division 1 / Division 3.
Eu = European – European Cup Winners Cup / Inter-Cities Fairs Cup / European Cup / World Club Championship.
FAC = FA Cup / Scottish FA Cup / Bass Irish Cup. **LC** = League Cup / Bells League Cup. **Tot** = Total.

		Res	Lge	FAC	LC	Tot
Jewish Guild	1974	-	4	-	-	4
Stockport County	1975 / 76	-	3	-	-	3
Cork Celtic	1975 / 76	-	3	-	-	3
Fulham	1976 / 77	1	32	2	3	38
	1977 / 78	-	10	-	-	10
Hibernian	1979 / 80	-	13	3	-	16
	1980 / 81	-	4	-	2	6
AFC Bournemouth	1982 / 83	-	5	-	-	5
Brisbane Lions	1983	-	4	-	-	4
Tobermore United	1983 / 84	-	-	1	-	1

		Regular Season	Play-offs	Totals
Los Angeles Aztecs	1976	23	1	24
	1977	20	5	25
	1978	12	-	12
Fort Lauderdale Strikers	1978	9	5	14
	1979	19		19
San Jose Earthquakes	1980	26	-	26
	1981	30	-	30
Indoor Season				
	1980 / 81	16		
	1981 / 82	5		

NORTHERN IRELAND					
	WCQ	ENQ	HIC	FRI	Total
	14	6	15	2	37
1964	2	-	3	1	6
1965	4	-	2	-	6
1966	-	1	-	-	1
1967	-	-	1	-	1
1968	1	-	-	-	1
1969	1	-	3	-	4
1970	-	1	3	-	4
1971	-	3	3	-	6
1972	1	1	-	-	2
1973	1	-	-	-	1
1974	-	-	-	-	-
1975	-	-	-	-	-
1976	2	-	-	-	2
1977	2	-	-	1	3

Key

WCQ = World Cup Qualifier
ENQ = European Nations Cup Qualifier
HIC = Home (British) International Championship
FRI = Friendly

	A	B	Yth	Res	Lge	Eu	FAC	LC	Tot
Manchester United	16	29	5	3	137	11	21	9	231
Jewish Guild	-	-	-	-	1	-	-	-	1
Stockport County	-	-	-	-	2	-	-	-	2
Cork Celtic	-	-	-	-	0	-	-	-	0
Fulham	-	-	-	-	8	-	0	2	10
Hibernian	-	-	-	-	3	-	0	0	3
AFC Bournemouth	-	-	-	-	0	-	-	-	0
Brisbane Lions	-	-	-	-	0	-	-	-	0
Tobermore United	-	-	-	-	-	-	0	-	0
Totals	16	29	5	3	151	11	21	11	247

	Regular Season		Play-offs	
	Goals	Assists	Goals	Assists
Los Angeles Aztecs	27	25	2	4
Fort Lauderdale Strikers	6	8	1	2
San Jose Earthquakes	21	21	-	-
San Jose Earthquakes (Indoor League)	33	42		

MANCHESTER UNITED									
	A	B	Yth	Res	Lge	Eu	FAC	LC	Tot
1961 / 62	2	10	-	-	-	-	-	-	12
1962 / 63	7	19	0	-	-	-	-	-	26
1963 / 64	7	-	5	3	4	0	2	-	21
1964 / 65	-	-	-	-	10	2	2	-	14
1965 / 66	-	-	-	-	9	4	3	-	16
1966 / 67	-	-	-	-	10	-	0	0	10
1967 / 68	-	-	-	-	28	3	1	-	32
1968 / 69	-	-	-	-	19	2	1	-	22
1969 / 70	-	-	-	-	15	-	6	2	23
1970 / 71	-	-	-	-	18	-	1	2	21
1971 / 72	-	-	-	-	18	-	5	3	26
1972 / 73	-	-	-	-	4	-	-	2	6
1973 / 74	-	-	-	0	2	-	-	-	2
Totals	16	29	5	3	137	11	21	9	231

		Res	Lge	FAC	LC	Tot
Jewish Guild	1974	-	1	-	-	1
Stockport County	1975 / 76	-	2	-	-	2
Cork Celtic	1975 / 76	-	0	-	-	0
Fulham	1976 / 77	0	6	0	2	8
	1977 / 78	-	2	-	-	2
Hibernian	1979 / 80	-	3	0	-	3
	1980 / 81	-	0	-	0	0
AFC Bournemouth	1982 / 83	-	0	-	-	0
Brisbane Lions	1983	-	0	-	-	0
Tobermore United	1983 / 84	-	-	0	-	0

		Regular Season		Play-offs	
		Goals	Assists	Goals	Assists
Los Angeles Aztecs	1976	15	7	0	0
	1977	11	18	2	4
	1978	1	0	-	-
Fort Lauderdale Strikers	1978	4	1	1	2
	1979	2	7	-	-
San Jose Earthquakes	1980	8	11	-	-
	1981	13	10	-	-
San Jose Earthquakes	1980 / 81	25	27		
(Indoor League)	1981 / 82	8	15		

NORTHERN IRELAND					
	WCQ	ENQ	HIC	FRI	Total
1964	1	0	0	0	1
1965	1	0	0	0	1
1966	0	0	0	0	0
1967	0	0	0	0	0
1968	1	0	0	0	1
1969	0	0	0	0	0
1970	0	0	1	0	1
1971	0	4	0	0	4
1972	0	0	0	0	0
1973	0	0	0	0	0
1974	-	-	-	-	-
1975	-	-	-	-	-
1976	0	0	0	0	0
1977	0	0	0	0	0
	3	4	1	0	8

Bibliography

Blessed – George Best, Ebury Press, 2002

Manchester United: A Complete Record 1878-1986 – Ian Morrison & Alan Shury, Breedon Books, 1986

Manchester United: The Forgotten Fixtures – Iain McCartney, Breedon Books, 2009

NASL: A Complete Record of the North American Soccer League – Colin Jose, Breedon Books, 1989

Rothman's Football Yearbook 1977 / 78, MacDonald and Jane's, 1977

Rothman's Football Yearbook 1978 / 79, MacDonald and Jane's, 1978

Rothman's Football Yearbook 1980 / 81, Queen Anne Press, 1980

Rothman's Football Yearbook 1981 / 82, Queen Anne Press, 1981

Rothman's Football Yearbook 1983 / 84, Rothman's / Queen Anne Press 1983